BADLANDS NATIONAL PARK, SOUTH DAKOTA

MOUNT RAINIER NATIONAL PARK, WASHINGTON

A *Guide to* **Our**

Federal Lands

GREEN MOUNTAIN NATIONAL FOREST, VERMONT

Introduction

Whether you are planning a long holiday or a short one, the federal lands of the United States offer an almost endless array of choices. Encompassing more than 700 million acres—nearly a third of the nation—this natural legacy preserves a variety of landforms, waterways, and ecological zones unmatched in any other country. From the subtropical swamps of Florida to the glacial wonderlands of Alaska, from meandering scenic drives to rugged mountain wilderness, there is truly something for everyone.

A companion to the National Geographic Society's book *Our Threatened Inheritance: Natural Treasures of the United States,* this guide is a unique compendium of federal areas of scenic and recreational importance that are open to the public. Its state-by-state entries are intended as a general aid in trip planning; they are necessarily brief, however, and travelers are urged, before setting out, to write or call personnel at the addresses noted in all listings. Local staffs in federal areas can supply prospective visitors with useful literature and up-to-date information on weather, campsite availability, and other variables to help make vacations relaxing and enjoyable.

We wish to thank the National Park Service, the U. S. Fish and Wildlife Service, the Bureau of Land Management, and the U. S. Forest Service for their generous assistance in compiling and reviewing the entries. With their cooperation, we selected the 664 federally owned areas described in this guide. They include:

> • 56 national parks, 57 national monuments (excluded were those of primarily historical interest), 4 national lakeshores, 11 national seashores, 19 national recreation areas, 6 national rivers or scenic riverways, 13 national preserves, and the Appalachian National Scenic Trail—all administered by the National Park Service (NPS);

> • 143 national forests, 19 national grasslands, and the Pacific Crest and Continental Divide National Scenic Trails—all administered by the Forest Service;

> • 257 national wildlife refuges, with varying official names, that are open to the public;

> • 76 areas of scenic and recreational interest within 46 Bureau of Land Management (BLM) districts. These less well known and often remote sites, administered for multiple uses, generally lack visitor facilities. Increased visitor use would threaten a few BLM areas covered in our book; those areas do not appear in the guide.

The guide is organized alphabetically by state, and federal areas in each state are listed alphabetically. If an area—a forest, for example—lies in more than one state, the main entry is usually under the state with the larger section; a cross-reference is given under the other state or states.

A map of each state provides a graphic overview of federal lands; numbers on the maps are keyed to specific entries, including cross-references, and indicate approximate locations. Colors—or, where the area is very small, symbols—denote the four general categories of federal lands:

red, or the symbol of an arrowhead (♦), for areas in the national park system;

green for national forests and grasslands;

blue, or the symbol of a goose in flight (➤), for national wildlife refuges;

gold for BLM districts, with a square symbol (▪) for each site.

Broken black lines indicate national scenic trails.

A number on a color-coded background, keyed to the map, precedes each entry on the left-hand side of the page. Here are listed the name of the area and its mailing address and telephone number. On the right is a capsule description of the area's terrain, vegetation, wildlife, and, if pertinent, points of cultural or historical interest. Recreational activities for which the area is well known may also be mentioned. Wilderness and primitive areas and wild and scenic rivers are usually noted as well. Such official designations denote lands and waters preserved as much as possible in a natural state. They are generally uninhabited, closed to motor vehicles and to commercial enterprise, and lacking in visitor facilities. For BLM areas, which often do not appear on road maps, brief directions from nearby towns may be given.

Below the general description, specific data are provided, including:

• acreage or, in the case of rivers and trails, miles;

• other state(s), if any, in which the area lies;

• access, if the area is inaccessible by automobile and can be entered only on foot or by boat, airplane, or some other means;

• visiting period, if the area is not open 24 hours a day year round, except for the usual Thanksgiving, Christmas, and New Year's Day closings;

• best time(s) to visit, and reasons, if relevant;

• fees, permits, and reservations, when required or recommended;

• source of visitor information, if obtainable from a place other than the address listed for the entry, and, if there is a visitor center, anything that it features—exhibits or tours, for example;

• number of rooms and campsites, if applicable, or, in some cases, the notation "primitive camping," which indicates the absence of facilities and marked-off sites;

• food services, when available, denoting eating facilities and/or stores where groceries may be purchased;

• tour bus or other conveyance, if provided within the area;

• food and lodging, only if available within a 15-mile radius;

• in some entries, additional important information concerning hazards, for example, or weather conditions not previously mentioned, or unusual situations requiring special preparation.

At the end of each entry, a series of symbols indicates the area's recreational offerings and facilities, and may include any combination of the following:

Backpacking or hiking—often, only hiking.

Boating—usually limited to sailboats, canoes, and the like; powerboat owners should check ahead.

Boat ramps—generally means that powerboats *are* permitted; sometimes only electric motors are allowed, or horsepower is limited.

Climbing—rock or mountain, and usually requiring special equipment.

Cycling—bicycles only.

Fishing—always requires a state license.

Horseback riding—usually, visitors must bring their own horses.

Hunting—always requires a state license.

Picnic areas.

Scenic or wildlife drives.

Skiing—cross-country or downhill; also may indicate other winter sports such as snowshoeing or bobsledding.

Swimming.

Provisions for the handicapped—varying widely from area to area.

Pets—permitted *on leashes* when this symbol appears; otherwise, not at all.

This guide introduces you to the many possibilities for recreation and learning that America's federal lands offer. Perhaps the most important—and least tangible—of these is the opportunity every visitor has to experience nature's wonders. Those who rush through a park, refuge, or forest at city speeds often forfeit that chance; those who leave behind the trappings of carelessness further the threat to our fragile natural heritage. Those who explore slowly and with care return home enriched and renewed.

Abbreviations of official designations used in this guide:

N.F.	National Forest
N.G.	National Grassland
N.H.P.	National Historical Park
N.L.	National Lakeshore
N.M.	National Monument
N.P.	National Park
N.R.	National River
N.R.A.	National Recreation Area
N.S.	National Seashore
N.S.R.	National Scenic Riverway(s)
N.S.T.	National Scenic Trail
N.W.R.	National Wildlife Refuge
W.M.A.	Wildlife Management Area
W.M.D.	Wetland Management District

DEWITT JONES

DELICATE ARCH IN ARCHES NATIONAL PARK, UTAH

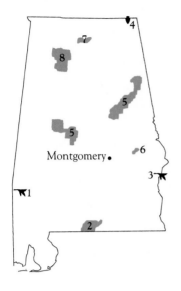

Montgomery.

Alabama

Meandering streams and shaded ponds promise fine fishing within Alabama's national forests. Bird watchers flock to Wheeler and Eufaula National Wildlife Refuges, where more than two hundred species have been sighted.

1 Choctaw N.W.R.
2704 Westside
  College Ave.
Jackson, AL 36545
(205) 246-3583

Bottomland hardwoods and farmland, with lakes and sloughs, along Tombigbee River. Numerous birds, including woodpeckers, wood ducks, and wild turkeys; also beavers and other fauna.

4,218 acres. Open dawn to dusk. Spring, fall best times. Refuge often flooded between Dec. and Apr.; sections closed much of year for waterfowl sanctuary or because of hazardous driving conditions. Food and lodging nearby.

2 Conecuh N.F.
1100 S. Three
  Notch St.
Andalusia, AL
36420
(205) 222-2555

Lush pine forests on coastal plain; ponds and streams; semi-tropical vegetation.

84,000 acres. Open 6 a.m.–10 p.m. Spring, fall best times. Entrance fee. Information at ranger station in Andalusia. 43 campsites. Food and lodging nearby.

3 Eufaula N.W.R.
Route 2, Box 97-B
Eufaula, AL 36027
(205) 687-4065

Marsh, woods, and uplands bordering Walter F. George Reservoir on Chattahoochee River. Wide range of bird-life, including herons, egrets, gallinules, wood ducks; also alligators, white-tailed deer.

11,160 acres, part in GA. Open dawn to dusk. Fall, winter, spring best times. Food and lodging nearby.

4 **Russell Cave N.M.**
Route 1, Box 175
Bridgeport, AL
35740
(205) 495-2672

Ancient Indian cave shelter in northeastern Alabama, continuously inhabited for at least 8,000 years.

310 acres. Open 8 a.m.–5 p.m. Guided tours and demonstrations available. Food and lodging nearby.

5 **Talladega N.F.**
1765 Highland Ave.
P.O. Box 40
Montgomery, AL
36101
(205) 832-7630

Mixed stands of hardwood and pine; mountains, valleys, and rocky cliffs. Scenic drive includes highest point in Alabama.

371,258 acres. User fee for developed areas. Information at ranger stations in Centreville, Heflin, and Talladega. Rooms; 168 campsites, most year-round. Food and lodging nearby.

6 **Tuskegee N.F.**
Route 1, Box 204
   AA
Tuskegee, AL
36083
(205) 727-2652

Hardwood and pine habitats on rolling hills midway between mountains and coast; trails; numerous small streams and creeks.

10,791 acres. Open 7:30 a.m.–4 p.m. Spring, summer best times. Information at ranger station in Tuskegee. Primitive camping. Food and lodging nearby.

7 **Wheeler N.W.R.**
P.O. Box 1643
Decatur, AL 35602
(205) 350-6639

Easternmost N.W.R. on lower Mississippi flyway; old river bed with backwater sloughs, woodlands, and fields along Tennessee River. Wheeler Reservoir attracts thousands of wintering ducks and Canada geese.

34,500 acres. Nov. 1–Feb. 1 best time. Reservations required for tour groups. Interpretive center. Food and lodging nearby.

8 **William B.**
   Bankhead N.F.
1765 Highland Ave.
Montgomery, AL
36107
(205) 832-7630

Noted for stands of virgin hardwood. Streams, lakes, and waterfalls; deep canyons and bluffs; wildlife refuge area.

179,539 acres. Summer best time. User fee. Information at ranger stations in Double Springs and Haleyville. 153 campsites. Food and lodging nearby.

Alaska

Awesome in magnitude and diverse in character, Alaska's federally owned lands comprise 256 million acres—more than one-third of the national total. From Mount McKinley, the continent's highest peak, to Arctic sand dunes, glacier-carved fjords, and richly varied wildlife, a wealth of natural treasures lures travelers to all parts of Alaska—a name derived from an Aleut Indian word meaning "great land." Wilderness remains the byword here, and trips require careful planning in a state where small planes, boats, or snowmobiles provide sole access to many remote areas. Mindful of the rigorous climate, most visitors prefer to travel in Alaska between May and September.

1 **Alaska Maritime**
 N.W.R.
P.O. Box 3069
Homer, AK 99603
(907) 235-6546

Approximately 2,500 islands—and 10 cliffs along the mainland—stretching 3,500 miles from the Arctic Ocean to the western end of the Aleutian Islands and to southeast Alaska. Habitat for some 30 million nesting seabirds and tens of thousands of sea otters, sea lions, seals, and other marine mammals. Refuge divided into 5 administrative units: Aleutian Islands, Chukchi Sea, Bering Sea, Alaska Peninsula, and Gulf of Alaska.

3,500,000 acres. May–Sept. best time. Permits required to land on certain islands. Information at Adak subheadquarters as well as at HQ in Homer. Primitive camping. Boat or plane charters can be arranged from Homer, Seward, Sandpoint, and other communities. Not all activities and facilities are available at all units.

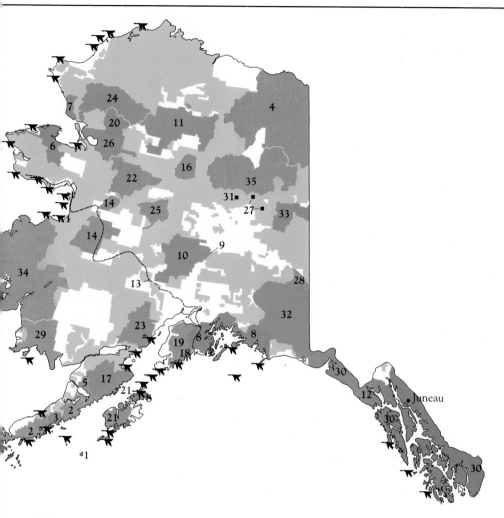

2   Alaska Peninsula N.W.R

1011 E. Tudor Rd.
Anchorage, AK
99503
(907) 246-3339

Rocky shores, rivers, lakes, and active volcanoes stretching along Pacific coast of Alaska Peninsula. Brown bears along salmon-filled streams; also moose, caribou, and wolves.

3,500,000 acres. June–Sept. best time. Information at Alaska Peninsula N.W.R., Box 277, King Salmon, AK 99613. Thorough advance planning required.

3 **Aniakchak N.M. and Preserve**
P.O. Box 7
King Salmon, AK
99613
(907) 246-3305

Aleutian caldera, 6 miles across, contains Surprise Lake, which drains into Aniakchak Wild River; volcano dormant for 50 years. Brown bears. Wildlife watching.

603,000 acres. Access entirely by air or by air and an arduous 10-mile walk. Mid-June–mid-Sept. best time. Permits required for backcountry use. Backcountry trails information from NPS, Alaska Regional Office, 540 W. 5th Ave., Rm. 202, Anchorage, AK 99501, or from Superintendent, Katmai N.P. and Preserve, King Salmon. Primitive camping; food should be obtained in Anchorage or King Salmon.

4 **Arctic N.W.R.**
101 12th Ave.
Box 20
Fairbanks, AK 99701
(907) 456-0250

Vast refuge extending north to the Arctic Ocean and east to Canada; encompasses spruce forests, meandering rivers, and snowcapped peaks of Brooks Range.

19,300,000 acres. Access by air or on foot. June–early Sept. best time. Information in Kaktouik. Primitive camping. Wilderness experience in truest sense: no visitor facilities, no roads.

5 **Becharof N.W.R.**
P.O. Box 277
King Salmon, AK
99613
(907) 246-3339

Surrounds Becharof Lake; bounded by gentle hills and tundra wetlands in north and volcanic mountains and Pacific Ocean in south and east. Recently (1977) active volcanoes; salmon-rich streams; brown bears, moose, and caribou. Severe weather.

1,200,000 acres. Access by chartered aircraft. June–Oct. best time. Primitive camping; no facilities.

6 **Bering Land Bridge National Preserve**
Box 220
General Delivery
Nome, AK 99762
(907) 443-2522

50 miles from Siberia, this remnant of the land bridge between Asia and North America abounds in arctic mammals and migratory birds. Eskimos here pursue traditional ways.

2,785,000 acres. Access by chartered aircraft. June best time. Information at NPS office, Kotzebue. Primitive camping. Site very isolated; arrive self-sufficient.

7 **Cape Krusenstern N.M.**
P.O. Box 287
Kotzebue, AK
99752
(907) 442-3890

6,000-year-old archaeological record of Eskimo life in northwestern Alaska; sites on beach ridges and coastal hills. Whales, seals, grizzlies, caribou, moose, waterfowl.

658,000 acres. Access by plane or boat from Kotzebue, 20 miles away. Mid-June–mid-Sept. best time. Consult staff at HQ in Kotzebue before visiting area. Primitive camping. Food and lodging in Kotzebue.

8 Chugach N.F.
2221 E. Northern
Lights Blvd.
Suite 238
Anchorage, AK
99508
(907) 279-5541

Region of fjords and glaciers, snowcapped peaks, alpine tundra, spruce and birch forests, secluded bays. Wildlife includes trumpeter swans, Canada geese, black and brown bears, Dall sheep, salmon.

6,210,710 acres. Reservations required for cabins. Visitor center at Portage Glacier. 36 cabins; 400 campsites, most open late May–early Sept. 2 winter sports areas. Food and lodging nearby.

9 Denali Highway
Bureau of Land
Management
4700 E. 72nd Ave.
Anchorage, AK
99507
(907) 267-1200

135-mile route from Paxson to Cantwell through landscape of mountains, lakes, rivers, and tundra. Vegetation includes lichens, berries, spruces; caribou, moose, and bears often sighted, as well as loons, terns, and graylings.

July best time. Road, much of it gravel, may be closed by snow Oct.–Apr. Food and lodging—in season—along the way; check with BLM's Glennallen Resource Area Office, Box 147, Glennallen, AK, for locations and other information. 37 campsites.

10 Denali N.P. and
Preserve
P.O. Box 9
McKinley Park, AK
99755
(907) 683-2294

North America's highest peak, Mount McKinley—or Denali, the "great one"—rises 20,230 feet in glaciered wilderness. Wildlife watching; bird watching in summer; dogsledding.

6,028,000 acres. Spring, summer, fall best times. Permits required for backcountry use. Visitor information center: interpretive talks and walks. 140 rooms; 225 campsites; food services; tour bus. Food and lodging nearby.

11 Gates of the Arctic
N.P. and Preserve
P.O. Box 74680
Fairbanks, AK 99707
(907) 456-0281

Tundra wilderness north of Arctic Circle. Diverse terrain of high, rugged peaks and steep valleys; lakes and rivers yet unnamed. Short, mild summers.

8,473,000 acres. Access by air. Summer best time. Information at NPS HQ, Fairbanks. Primitive camping. Guided and outfitted trips available. Food and lodging nearby.

KATMAI NATIONAL PARK AND PRESERVE, ALASKA

12 **Glacier Bay N.P.**
and Preserve
Gustavus, AK 99826
(907) 697-3341

Large tidewater glaciers on Alaska's southeastern coast. Opportunity to see glacial geology in action; also plant and animal succession.

3,234,000 acres. Access by plane or boat from Juneau; bus from Gustavus Airfield to Bartlett Cove. May–Sept. best time. Permits required for boating. Information and rental kayaks at Bartlett Cove; evening programs; interpretive programs and hikes. 55 rooms; 30 campsites; food services. Extreme caution advised on glacial surfaces. Food and lodging in Gustavus.

13 **Iditarod National**
Historic Trail
Bureau of Land
Management
4700 E. 72nd Ave.
Anchorage, AK 99507
(907) 267-1200

Network of trails between Seward and Nome crosses mountains and tundra on federal, state, Native, and privately owned lands. Route of gold seekers, other adventurers; abandoned towns; streams, marshes, and muskeg; wild flowers; salmon, birds.

2,300 miles. Summer best time for hiking; Iditarod Dogsled Race in Mar. Only southern section between Seward and Anchorage accessible by road. Information at Chugach N.F. and state parks. Primitive camping.

14 **Innoko N.W.R.**
McGrath General
Delivery
McGrath, AK 99741
(907) 524-3251

Mainly wetlands in central Yukon River Valley; includes some Yukon River islands, most of Innoko River basin, and Kaiyuh Flats. Nesting site for waterfowl; home to moose, caribou, wolves, black bears, and furbearers.

3,850,000 acres. Late spring, summer best times. Primitive camping.

15 **Izembek N.W.R.**
Pouch 2
Cold Bay, AK 99571
(907) 532-2445

Wetlands, lagoons, and volcanic mountains toward southern end of Alaska Peninsula. Home to world's total population of black brants in fall; immense gatherings of emperor and Canada geese; pintail, mallard, and teal ducks; also mammals such as brown bears, wolves, caribou.

321,000 acres. Access by plane or boat. May, Oct. best times.

16 **Kanuti N.W.R.**
101 12th Ave.
Box 20
Fairbanks, AK 99701
(907) 456-0329

Wide, rolling plain with spruce and fir forest, lakes, ponds, streams, and marshes. Waterfowl abound, including white-footed and Canada geese and several duck species; also Arctic caribou, moose, black bears, and wolves.

1,430,000 acres. Summer best time. Primitive camping. No roads to or on refuge; several streams leading west to refuge from Dalton Hwy. Marshy area, not suitable for hiking or backpacking.

17 Katmai N.P. and Preserve
P.O. Box 7
King Salmon, AK 99613
(907) 246-3305

Wilderness encompassing Valley of Ten Thousand Smokes and ice-covered Aleutian Range; lakes, rivers, and alpine streams; coastal fjords and bays. Abundant wildlife includes brown bears, marine mammals, salmon.

4,093,000 acres. Access by commercial aircraft in summer only; charter flights year round. June–early Sept. best time. Backcountry permits required. Information at Brooks Camp Ranger Station; lectures. 15 rooms; 28 campsites; food services; tour bus. Food and lodging in King Salmon and Brooks River.

18 Kenai Fjords N.P.
P.O. Box 1727
Seward, AK 99664
(907) 224-3874

Ice fields and glaciers; coastal fjords harboring seabirds, whales, porpoises, sea otters, sea lions, and seals. Cool, rainy climate.

669,000 acres. Summer best time. Information at Chamber of Commerce, Seward, AK 99664, or Homer, AK 99603. Primitive camping. Food and lodging nearby.

19 Kenai N.W.R.
P.O. Box 2139
Soldotna, AK 99669
(907) 262-7021

Meadows, hills, forests, and some 4,000 lakes southwest of Anchorage. Moose herds; bears, mountain goats, and Dall sheep; loons, ptarmigans, and spruce grouse; salmon in vast network of streams and rivers. 200 miles of hiking trails; 200 miles of canoe trails.

2,000,000 acres. Spring, summer, fall best times. Visitor center in Soldotna; information station at Mile 58, Sterling Hwy., open Memorial Day–Labor Day. 300 campsites. Food and lodging nearby.

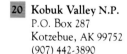

20 Kobuk Valley N.P.
P.O. Box 287
Kotzebue, AK 99752
(907) 442-3890

River valley north of Arctic Circle. Archaeological sites; 100-foot Great Kobuk Sand Dunes. Moose, brown and black bears, wolves, caribou, foxes, waterfowl.

1,750,000 acres. Access by plane or boat. Feb.–Apr., June–Sept. best times. Write or call NPS office in Kotzebue before planning trip. Primitive camping.

21 Kodiak N.W.R.
P.O. Box 825
Kodiak, AK 99615
(907) 486-3325

Island sanctuary for huge Kodiak bears off southwest shore of Alaska; Pacific salmon spawn in streams and rivers; also nesting eagles and migrating seabirds such as shearwaters, cormorants, and kittiwakes. Weather frequently severe.

1,865,000 acres. Access by plane or boat. Spring, summer, fall best times. Visitor center. 11 cabins, reservations required; primitive camping. Food and lodging nearby.

22 Koyukuk N.W.R.
Box 287
Galena, AK 99471
(907) 656-1231

Thick spruce forests, with rivers, streams, lakes, ponds, and sloughs, on vast floodplain. Flocks of ducks and white-fronted geese; shorebirds nesting in wetlands; trumpeter swan nesting area.

3,550,000 acres. Late summer best time. Primitive camping.

23 Lake Clark N.P. and Preserve
701 C St.
Box 61
Anchorage, AK 99513
(907) 271-3751

Diverse area encompassing boggy wetlands, alpine tundra, glaciers, rugged mountains, and coastal forests. Wildlife includes moose, Dall sheep, caribou, brown and black bears. White-water rafting.

4,045,000 acres. Access by small aircraft. June–Sept. best time. Rooms; primitive camping; food services. Food and lodging nearby.

24 Noatak National Preserve
P.O. Box 287
Kotzebue, AK 99752
(907) 442-3890

Mountain-flanked river basin with ancient archaeological sites. Grand Canyon of the Noatak provides migration route for caribou. Spectacular wild flowers.

6,559,000 acres. Access by plane or boat. Summer best time. Write or call NPS office in Kotzebue before planning trip. Primitive camping. Food and lodging in Kotzebue.

25 Nowitna N.W.R.
Box 287
Galena, AK 99741
(907) 656-1231

Forested lowlands along Nowitna Wild and Scenic River and Yukon River. Fishes and waterfowl such as trumpeter swans thrive here.

1,560,000 acres. Summer best time. Remote refuge, no services; write or call refuge office before planning trip. Primitive camping.

26 Selawik N.W.R.
Box 270
Kotzebue, AK 99752
(907) 442-3799

Lakes along delta coast in northwest Alaska; farther inland, lowlands with lakes, streams, and marshes; uplands to north and south. Wintering herd of Arctic caribou; large numbers of water birds.

2,150,000 acres. Summer best time. Primitive camping. Weather and insects can be very bad.

27 Steese National Conservation Area
Bureau of Land Management
Box 1150
Fairbanks, AK 99707
(907) 356-5302

Hiking trails lead away from Steese Highway, which bisects this scenic area. Parts of Steese-Fortymile caribou herd can be observed during migrations in June and Sept. Good views of "midnight sun" from Eagle Summit; sunlight 24 hours a day in June. Wild flowers.

1,250,000 acres. June–Aug. best time. Hwy. closed at Eagle Summit Nov.–May. Cabins; primitive camping.

28 Tetlin N.W.R.
Box 155
Tok, AK 99780
(907) 883-5312

Rolling plain with marshes, ponds, lakes, forest, and hills; touches Canadian border south of Alaska Highway. More than 15 duck species; great numbers of sandhill cranes.

700,000 acres. Spring, summer, fall best times. Primitive camping.

29 Togiak N.W.R.
P.O. Box 10201
Dillingham, AK 99576
(907) 842-1063

Wide glacial valleys cut across Ahklun Mountains of southwest Alaska. Seabird nesting cliffs; resting and breeding site for birds such as pintails, common scoters, and oldsquaws; important spawning ground for Bristol Bay salmon; brown bears.

4,105,000 acres. Access by air. Summer best time. Primitive camping.

30 Tongass N.F.
P.O. Box 309
Petersburg, AK 99833
(907) 772-3841

Largest N.F. unit, encompassing rugged coastal area with rain forests of moss-draped spruce and hemlock; bogs with colorful wild flowers; inland waterways. Glacier Observatory at Lake Mendenhall.

16,832,727 acres. Many areas accessible only by plane or boat. Reservations required for cabins. Information at Forest Service offices in Ketchikan, Petersburg, and Sitka and at ranger work centers in Craig, Juneau, Thorn Bay, Wrangell, and Yakutat. 130 cabins; 171 campsites, open May–Oct.; food services. Food and lodging nearby.

31 White Mountain N.R.A.
Bureau of Land Management
Box 1150
Fairbanks, AK 99707
(907) 356-5302

Jagged limestone cliffs and peaks of White Mountains contrast with surrounding green, rolling hills. Beaver Creek, designated a wild river, flows through area for 111 miles. Moose, bears, caribou, wolves, and Dall sheep.

1,000,000 acres. Possible to boat in, but difficult to boat out; visitors should arrange to have a bush plane pick them up. Rivers freeze in Oct., thaw in May. Late May–early June for wild flowers. 2 cabins; primitive camping.

32 Wrangell-St. Elias N.P. and Preserve
P.O. Box 29
Glennallen, AK 99588
(907) 822-5234

Largest NPS unit, with diverse terrain of ice-clad peaks, deep canyons, tundra uplands, forested lowlands; rich in wildlife. Air tours.

13,188,000 acres. Summer best time. Permits required for helicopter access. Information at Mile 105½, Richardson Hwy. Primitive camping; food services. 3 developed campgrounds on park periphery. Food and lodging nearby.

33 Yukon-Charley Rivers National Preserve
P.O. Box 64
Eagle, AK 99738
(907) 547-2233

Scenic and historic region of rivers, forested valleys, tundra uplands. Ruins of Yukon gold rush camps. White-water canoeing and rafting; wildlife watching.

2,527,000 acres. Summer best time. Primitive camping. Food and lodging in Eagle and Circle.

34 Yukon Delta N.W.R.
P.O. Box 346
Bethel, AK 99559
(907) 543-3151

Largest N.W.R. unit, encompassing delta plains of Yukon and Kuskokwim Rivers in western Alaska; cliffs, craters, and sand dunes of Nunivak Island. Great gatherings of waterfowl, shorebirds, and seabirds.

19,624,458 acres. Spring, summer, fall best times. Primitive camping.

35 Yukon Flats N.W.R.
101 12th Ave.
Box 20
Fairbanks, AK 99701
(907) 456-0250

Basin wetlands 100 miles north of Fairbanks, rimmed by hills and containing some 2,500 miles of streams and rivers. Huge numbers of ducks and geese; also sandhill cranes, loons, other birds; moose, bears, caribou, and Dall sheep.

8,630,000 acres. Extremely isolated; access by plane or boat. Spring, summer, fall best times. Primitive camping.

DENALI NATIONAL PARK AND PRESERVE, ALASKA

GRAND CANYON NATIONAL PARK, ARIZONA

Arizona

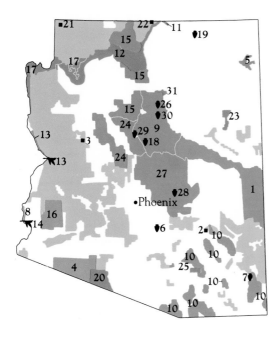

"One of the great sights which every American . . . should see," in Theodore Roosevelt's words, the Grand Canyon epitomizes Arizona's natural wonders. Geologic eons and a wide range of climatic zones are in evidence here and throughout the state; ancient Indian ruins and 20th-century reservoirs attest human ingenuity in a challenging environment. For the visitor, seasonal considerations loom large: snow often closes roads to the Grand Canyon's spectacular North Rim from mid-October through mid-May; Sonoran Desert hillsides abloom with wild flowers in spring swelter in summer.

---

1 Apache-Sitgreaves N.F.
P.O. Box 640
Springerville, AZ 85938
(602) 333-4301

Encompasses ponderosa pine forest on south edge of Colorado Plateau and mountain-meadow country of the White Mountains. Scenic drives along Mogollon Rim and Coronado Trail. Streams and lakes offer many recreational opportunities.

2,619,387 acres, part in NM. Apr.–Oct. best time. Reservations required for Los Burros campground. Visitor center at Big Lake. 860 campsites; food services. Food and lodging nearby.

2 Aravaipa Canyon and Primitive Area
Bureau of Land Management
425 East 4th St.
Safford, AZ 85546
(602) 428-4040

Stream flows at base of 1,000-foot cliffs. Desert plants contrast with riparian vegetation; wildlife includes rattlesnakes, desert bighorn sheep, and more than 150 bird species.

6,899 acres. Spring, fall best times. Visitor centers at east and west administrative sites. Primitive camping.

3 Burro Creek
Bureau of Land
  Management
2475 Beverly
  Ave.
Kingman, AZ 86401
(602) 757-4011

Area of floodplains, canyons, and desert. Diverse plants, including saguaros, cottonwoods, and willows; wide variety of birds.

37,146 acres. Spring, fall best times. 50 campsites. Food and lodging nearby.

**4 Cabeza Prieta
  N.W.R.**
P.O. Box 418
Ajo, AZ 85321
(602) 387-6483

Rugged, remote desert and mountain region set aside to protect bighorn sheep and Sonoran pronghorns. Splendid desert flowers during moist periods in spring. Luke Air Force Range overlies part of refuge.

860,000 acres. Open to public 24 hours a day when not in use by military. Spring, fall, winter best times. Entry permits required from refuge HQ; permits required for photography from refuge blinds. Primitive camping. 4-wheel-drive vehicles recommended for primitive roads; carry emergency food, water, spare tire. Food and lodging nearby.

**5 Canyon de Chelly
  N.M.**
P.O. Box 588
Chinle, AZ 86503
(602) 674-5436

Ruins of ancient Indian cliff dwellings. Red-rock canyons, 1,000 feet deep, are part of Navajo Reservation.

83,840 acres. Spring, fall best times. Permits required for entrance to canyons; fees for guide services for hiking and 4-wheel driving; reservations required for group campsites. Visitor center in Chinle: exhibits, talks. 30 rooms; 100 campsites; food services. Jeep tours available. Food and lodging nearby.

6 Casa Grande N.M.
P.O. Box 518
Coolidge, AZ 85228
(602) 723-3172

Located in Coolidge, the ruins of a Hohokam village built around 1300 contain a massive caliche structure known as Casa Grande.

472 acres. Open 7 a.m.–6 p.m. Oct.–May best time. Entrance fee. Visitor center: talks, exhibits, walking tours. Be prepared for intense heat; watch out for cactus spines and poisonous animals. Food and lodging nearby.

7 Chiricahua N.M.
Dos Cabezas Route
Box 6500
Willcox, AZ 85643
(602) 824-3560

Rock formations in volcanic region; spires and pillars created by volcanic activity and shaped by erosion.

11,049 acres. Open 8 a.m.–5 p.m. Apr.–May, Sept.–Nov. best times. Entrance fee. Visitor center: exhibits, auto tours, campfire programs. 26 campsites.

8 Cibola N.W.R.
P.O. Box AP
Blythe, CA 92225
(602) 857-3262

Alluvial riverbed bordering lower Colorado River; lush stands of salt cedar, mesquite, and arrowwood, ringed by farmland feeding flocks of migrating waterfowl.

16,627 acres, part in CA. Open daylight hours. Nov.–Mar. best time. Food and lodging nearby.

9 Coconino N.F.
2323 E. Greenlaw
   La.
Flagstaff, AZ 86001
(602) 527-7400

Scenery includes stands of ponderosa pine; ancient San Francisco Peaks; buttes and plateaus; Oak Creek Canyon; lakes and flower-strewn meadows; remains of prehistoric settlements. Sycamore Canyon Wilderness Area.

1,835,705 acres. Information at ranger stations in Blue Ridge, Flagstaff, Happy Jack, Rimrock, and Sedona. 544 campsites, most open May–Sept. Winter sports area. Food and lodging nearby.

10 Coronado N.F.
301 W. Congress St.
Tucson, AZ 85701
(602) 629-6483

Rugged mountains rise abruptly from surrounding desert. Fir trees and cactuses; streams and lakes; canyons. Chiricahua, Galiuro, and Pusch Ridge Wilderness Areas. Bird watching.

1,780,196 acres, part in NM. Reservations required for Spencer Canyon camping area and Rose Canyon picnic area. Visitor center at Sabino Canyon; information also at Palisades Ranger Station; exhibits. 416 campsites, many year-round; food services. Carry water in backcountry. Food and lodging nearby.

11 Glen Canyon N.R.A.

see Utah

12 Grand Canyon N.P.
P.O. Box 129
Grand Canyon, AZ 86023
(602) 638-2411

Mile-deep Grand Canyon of the Colorado, world's largest gorge. Succession of peaks, mesas, and buttes; colored rock layers representing nearly 1.5 billion years of the earth's history. Mule rides; rim drives; river float trips; scenic flights. Strenuous climb to and from canyon floor.

1,218,375 acres. South Rim open year round; North Rim, mid-May–mid-Oct. Entrance fee; permits and reservations required for backcountry camping; reservations only for Mather Campground in summer. South Rim Visitor Center; North Rim Information Station; exhibits. 890 rooms; 287 campsites; food services; tour bus. Food and lodging nearby.

ORGAN PIPE CACTUS NATIONAL MONUMENT, ARIZONA

13 Havasu N.W.R.
1406 Bailey Ave.
Box A
Needles, CA 92363
(619) 326-3853

Sheer cliffs jut above 18-mile-long Topock Gorge unit, where night herons visit. Yuma clapper rails nest within 4,000-acre Topock Marsh unit. Bill Williams unit encompasses thick forest of willows and 50-foot cottonwoods, high, stony desert, and delta land.

45,851 acres, part in CA. Late fall–early spring best time. Primitive camping. Food and lodging nearby.

14 Imperial N.W.R.
P.O. Box 2217
Martinez Lake, AZ 85364
(602) 783-3400

Waterside brush and rugged uplands bound 30-mile stretch of Colorado River. Great blue herons, snowy and great egrets, and endangered Yuma clapper rails along banks; roadrunners and desert tortoises in desert uplands.

25,764 acres, part in CA. Open 7 a.m.–3:30 p.m. Mid-Oct.–late May best time. Food and lodging nearby.

15 Kaibab N.F.
800 S. 6th St.
Williams, AZ 86046
(602) 635-2681

On both sides of Grand Canyon. Pine, fir, spruce, and aspen; geologic formations. Wildlife includes rare Kaibab squirrels, mule deer, and bison.

1,556,432 acres. Winter access limited by snow. Visitor center at Jacob Lake. 194 rooms; 303 campsites; most developed camping areas open May–Oct.; food services in season; boat rentals.

16 Kofa N.W.R.
P.O. Box 6290
Yuma, AZ 85364
(602) 783-7861

Mountain peaks thrust above hills, canyons, and desert floor. Desert bighorn sheep often spotted atop ridges; golden eagles breed in Kofa Mountains; swifts and thrashers commonly sighted.

660,000 acres. Nov.–Apr. best time. Camping throughout refuge. Food nearby.

17 Lake Mead N.R.A. *see* Nevada

18 Montezuma Castle N.M.
P.O. Box 219
Camp Verde, AZ 86322
(602) 567-3322

Archaeological site includes one of the best preserved prehistoric cliff dwellings in U. S.

850 acres. Open 7 a.m.–7 p.m. from June to Sept.; 8 a.m.–5 p.m. rest of year. Entrance fee. Visitor center: exhibits. Food and lodging nearby.

19 Navajo N.M.
Tonalea, AZ 86044
(602) 672-2366

Cliff dwellings in sandstone alcoves on Navajo Reservation. Ruins consist of Betatakin, Keet Seel, and Inscription House, which is closed to the public.

360 acres. May–mid-Sept. best time. Trails into canyon closed after Sept. Registration required for ranger-led tours into canyon and ruins; reservations required to enter Keet Seel. Visitor center: exhibits; evening programs in summer. 30 campsites. Food nearby.

20 Organ Pipe Cactus N.M.
Route 1, Box 100
Ajo, AZ 85321
(602) 387-6849

Desert region of unique interest to botanists, ornithologists, zoologists; plants and animals found nowhere else in U. S.

330,600 acres. Nov.–Apr. best time. Permits required for backcountry use; reservations for groups. Visitor center, 17 miles south of park entrance: lectures. 208 campsites. Food and lodging nearby.

21 Paiute Primitive Area
Bureau of Land Management
196 E. Tabernacle
St. George, UT 84770
(801) 673-3545

Includes Mount Bangs, only named peak in rugged Virgin Mountains; canyons; springs. Diverse vegetation, from Mojave Desert cactuses to Douglas fir in high country. 20 miles southwest of St. George.

35,092 acres. Spring, fall best times. Primitive camping.

22 Paria Canyon Primitive Area

see Utah

23 Petrified Forest N.P.
Petrified Forest National Park, AZ 86028
(602) 524-6228

Multicolored rock surfaces of the Painted Desert; petrified trees, including giant Old Faithful. Indian ruins; Agate House, built of petrified logs.

93,493 acres. Open 6 a.m.–7 p.m. in summer; 7–6 in spring and fall; 8–5 in winter; occasional closings because of heavy snow or icy roads. Entrance fee; backcountry permits required. Painted Desert Visitor Center; Rainbow Forest Museum; interpretative talks, films, exhibits. Primitive camping, limited to 50,260 acres of wilderness area, permits required; food services; tour bus.

24 Prescott N.F.
344 S. Cortez St.
Prescott, AZ 86301
(602) 445-1762

Land of mountains, valleys, and desert. Varied plant life, from ponderosa pine to chaparral. Sycamore Canyon and Pine Mountain Wilderness Areas; Jerome, largest ghost town in U. S.

1,237,079 acres. Group permits and reservations required for Upper Wolf Creek camping area. Information at ranger stations in Camp Verde, Chino Valley, and Prescott and at Crown King work center. 299 campsites, some year-round; food services. Food and lodging nearby.

25 Saguaro N.M.
Old Spanish Trail
Route 8, Box 695
Tucson, AZ 85730
(602) 298-2036

Forests of giant saguaro cactuses in both Rincon Mountain and Tucson Mountain units; coniferous forest in Rincon only. Wildlife includes coyotes, deer, javelinas, lizards, snakes; bird watching.

83,576 acres. Rincon Mt. unit open 8 a.m. to sunset; Tucson Mt. unit open 24 hours. Spring, fall best times. Entrance fee for Rincon; permits required for overnight backcountry use. HQ and visitor center in Rincon Mt. unit; information center and visitor center in Tucson Mt. unit. Tour bus. Arizona-Sonora Desert Museum nearby. Food and lodging in Tucson.

Sitgreaves N.F.

see **Apache-Sitgreaves N.F.**

26 Sunset Crater N.M.
Route 3, Box 149
Flagstaff, AZ 86001
(602) 526-1586

Colorful crater, stained red and orange, formed 900 years ago. Lava Flow trail leads to crawlway caves containing ice formations.

3,040 acres. Open 8 a.m.–5 p.m.; 7 a.m.–7 p.m. in summer. Spring, summer, fall best times. Often closed by snow in winter. Visitor center: audiovisual programs, exhibits; campfire programs in summer. 44 campsites.

27 Tonto N.F.
P.O. Box 29070
Phoenix, AZ 85038
(602) 261-3205

Sonoran Desert; rugged mountains, winding canyons, and stands of pine and fir. 6 man-made lakes; 800 miles of trails. Mazatzal, Pine Mountain, Sierra Ancha, and Superstition Wilderness Areas.

2,874,500 acres. Summer, fall best times for higher elevations; fall, winter, spring for lower. Reservations required for group campsites. Information at ranger stations in Carefree, Globe, Mesa, Payson, Roosevelt, and Young. 491 campsites; food services. Food and lodging nearby.

28 Tonto N.M.
P.O. Box 707
Roosevelt, AZ 85545
(602) 467-2241

Well-preserved cliff dwellings inside huge natural cave in canyon wall; occupied by Salado Indian farmers in the 14th century.

1,120 acres. Open 8 a.m.–5 p.m.; trail to Lower Ruin closes at 4 p.m. Oct.–June best time. Entrance fee; reservations required for Upper Ruin (5 days' notice). Visitor center: interpretive exhibits, slide program, observation deck. Hazardous terrain; stay on trails. Food and lodging nearby.

29 Tuzigoot N.M.
P.O. Box 68
Clarkdale, AZ 86324
(602) 634-5564

Ruins of Indian village with 92 rooms on hilltop overlooking Verde River Valley; occupied 1125–1400.

849 acres. Open 8 a.m.–5 p.m. Spring, summer, fall best times. Entrance fee. Visitor center: museum exhibits; self-guided trail. Food and lodging nearby.

30 Walnut Canyon N.M.
Route 1, Box 25
Flagstaff, AZ 86001
(602) 526-3367

Ruins of some 300 cliff dwellings built by Sinagua Indians more than 800 years ago in the limestone canyon walls. Self-guided trails.

2,249 acres. Open 7 a.m.–7 p.m. Memorial Day–Labor Day; 8 a.m.–5 p.m. rest of year. Entrance fee. Visitor center: exhibits. Walking off designated trails is forbidden. Food and lodging nearby.

31 Wupatki N.M.
Tuba Star Route
Flagstaff, AZ 86001
(602) 774-7000

Ruins of prehistoric dwellings made of native red sandstone. Several large pueblo sites dating to the 12th century, including a 200-room pueblo with amphitheater and ball court. Builders believed to be ancestors of Hopis.

35,253 acres. Wupatki Visitor Center. Bonito campground near Sunset Crater administered by NPS; 44 campsites, open Apr. 1–Nov. 15.

Arkansas

With its old-time resort atmosphere, Hot Springs National Park attracts health-seekers who take the waters at numerous bathhouses. Others take to scenic rivers, streams, and bayous by canoe to explore fertile bottomlands and Ozark bluffs in Arkansas' national forests and wildlife refuges.

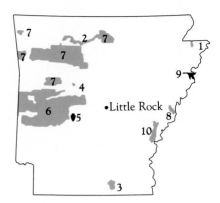

1 Big Lake N.W.R.
P.O. Box 67
Big Lake, AR 72442
(501) 564-2429

Winding creeks and open water, virgin cypress-tupelo swamp, and flooded woodland—all bounding Big Lake. Most duck species that travel the Mississippi flyway, plus songbirds such as Lincoln's sparrows and warbling vireos.

11,038 acres. Open dawn to dusk. Spring, fall best times. Information at refuge HQ, 2 miles east of Manila on Hwy. 18. Food and lodging nearby.

2 Buffalo N.R.
P.O. Box 1173
Harrison, AR 72601
(501) 741-5443

Wild, free-flowing river coursing 148 miles through Ozark hills; 132 miles are within park. On upper reaches, white-water kayaking past hardwood forests and limestone bluffs.

87,883 acres. Fall, winter best times. Information at several centers and at HQ; interpretive exhibits, campfire programs, guided walks, canoe trips. Rooms; 118 campsites; food services. Food and lodging nearby.

3 Felsenthal N.W.R.
P.O. Box 279
Crossett, AR 71635
(501) 364-8700

Bottomland hardwoods, open water, and outlying pine forests, with sloughs; lakes and juncture of 2 rivers. Waterfowl, deer, beavers, alligators, and other species.

65,000 acres. Winter, spring best times. Refuge periodically flooded. Primitive camping. Food and lodging nearby.

4 Holla Bend N.W.R.
P.O. Box 1043
Russellville, AR 72801
(501) 968-2800

Between Ozark Mountains in north and Ouachita Mountains in south. Home to bald eagles in winter; great flocks of waterfowl from late autumn through January.

4,083 acres. Open dawn to dusk. Fall, winter, early spring best times. Food and lodging nearby.

5 **Hot Springs N.P.**
P.O. Box 1860
Hot Springs, AR
71901
(501) 624-3383

47 hot springs offer warm relaxation of thermal bathing. Tranquil woodland provides habitat for 150 species of birds; wild flowers.

4,826 acres. Open 8 a.m.–5 p.m. Fee for bathhouse use. Visitor center at Central and Reserve Aves.; audiovisual and interpretive tours; campfire programs and exhibits at ranger station. 47 campsites; campers must first register at campground office. Campfires permitted only at specified sites. Food and lodging nearby.

6 **Ouachita N.F.**
P.O. Box 1270
Federal Building
Hot Springs
  National Park,
AR 71902
(501) 321-5202

Rolling, forested mountains, scenic lakes, and streams. Dense stands of oak, hickory, maple, gum, and dogwood provide brilliant fall color. Float trips on Ouachita River. 175-mile Ouachita National Recreation Trail.

1,585,264 acres, part in OK. Mid-Oct.–Nov. 1 for fall foliage. Reservations needed for group camping. Visitor centers at both ends of Talimena Scenic Drive; Kerr Arboretum and Nature Center at midpoint; exhibits. 550 campsites, many year-round. Food and lodging nearby.

7 **Ozark N.F.**
P.O. Box 1008
Russellville, AR
72801
(501) 968-2354

Quiet rivers and small streams winding among rock bluffs and oak, hickory, and pine forests. Lakes and waterfalls; natural bridges. Upper Buffalo Wilderness. Float trips; tours of Blanchard Springs Caverns.

1,119,000 acres. May–Oct. best time. Information at ranger stations in Clarksville, Hector, Jasper, Mountain View, Ozark, and Paris. 13 cabins; 278 campsites. Food and lodging nearby.

8 **St. Francis N.F.**
P.O. Box 1008
Russellville, AR
72801
(501) 968-2354

Stands of hardwood on Crowley's Ridge and in fertile bottomlands of Mississippi Delta. Excellent fishing in Bear Creek Lake.

20,946 acres. May–Dec. best time. Information at ranger station in Marianna. 53 campsites; check with HQ to be sure they are open. Food and lodging nearby.

9 **Wapanocca N.W.R.**
P.O. Box 279
Turrell, AR 72384
(501) 343-2595

Bottomland hardwood region with cypress-willow swamp. Winter habitat for waterfowl such as mallards and Canada geese; nesting habitat for wood ducks; numerous songbirds and birds of prey.

5,484 acres. Open dawn to dusk. Fall, winter, spring best times. Food and lodging nearby.

10 **White River N.W.R.**
P.O. Box 308
DeWitt, AR 72042
(501) 946-1468

Some 170 natural lakes and 125 miles of streams and bayous spread across mixed bottomland hardwood forests. Abundant white-tailed deer and wild turkeys; numerous songbirds.

112,348 acres. Open Mar. 1–Oct. 31. Spring, fall best times. 23 campsites, open Mar.–Oct. Food and lodging nearby.

OZARK NATIONAL FOREST, ARKANSAS

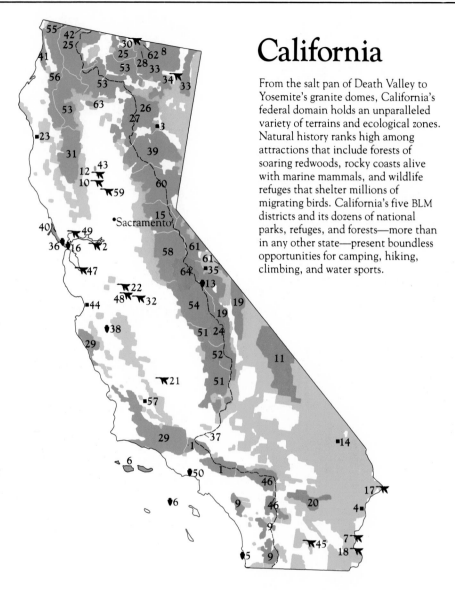

California

From the salt pan of Death Valley to Yosemite's granite domes, California's federal domain holds an unparalleled variety of terrains and ecological zones. Natural history ranks high among attractions that include forests of soaring redwoods, rocky coasts alive with marine mammals, and wildlife refuges that shelter millions of migrating birds. California's five BLM districts and its dozens of national parks, refuges, and forests—more than in any other state—present boundless opportunities for camping, hiking, climbing, and water sports.

1 **Angeles N.F.**
150 S. Los Robles
Suite 300
Pasadena, CA 91101
(818) 577-0050

Steep mountains covered with chaparral, woody shrubs, and stands of pine and fir. San Gabriel Wilderness.

653,862 acres. May–June best time. Permits required for wilderness area; reservations available for special campground for handicapped. 3 visitor centers, open Thurs.–Mon. 1,500 campsites; food services. Food and lodging nearby.

2 Antioch Dunes N.W.R.
P.O. Box 524
Newark, CA 94560
(415) 792-0222

First refuge established to protect endangered plants and insects, on stabilized grass-covered sand dunes along San Joaquin River. Species include Lange's metalmark butterfly, Contra Costa wallflower, Antioch Dunes evening primrose; also unique reptiles.

55 acres. Open daylight hours. Late winter, spring best times. Information at San Francisco Bay N.W.R.

3 Bizz Johnson Trail
Bureau of Land Management
P.O. Box 1090
2545 Riverside Dr.
Susanville, CA 96130
(916) 257-5381

Recreational trail follows old Fernley and Lassen Railroad tracks through scenic Susan River canyon and forests of the Sierra Nevada and the Cascade Range. Abundant and varied wildlife.

25 miles. Fire permits required June–Oct. Primitive camping. Food and lodging nearby.

4 Blythe Intaglios
Bureau of Land Management
P.O. Box 5680
Yuma, AZ 85364
(602) 726-6300

Six ancient figures engraved in desert gravel by Indians of Colorado River Valley. Largest manlike figure is 171 feet long; also animal forms. 15 miles north of Blythe.

2 acres. Oct.–May best time.

5 Cabrillo N.M.
P.O. Box 6670
San Diego, CA 92106
(619) 293-5450

Park commemorates Juan Rodriquez Cabrillo, discoverer of California in 1542. Includes Old Point Loma Lighthouse; tide pools; bayside trail through chaparral. Whale watching in winter.

144 acres. Open 9 a.m.–5:15 p.m. Visitor center: interpretive exhibits, audiovisual programs. Food and lodging nearby.

Calaveras Big Tree N.F.

see **Stanislaus N.F.**

6 Channel Islands N.P.
1901 Spinnaker Dr.
Ventura, CA 93001
(805) 644-8262

Island chain includes Anacapa, Santa Barbara, San Miguel, Santa Cruz, and Santa Rosa. Haven for marine mammals and seabirds. Scuba diving; snorkeling; boat excursions.

249,515 acres. Access by boat. San Miguel, Anacapa, and Santa Barbara open dawn to dusk. Permits required for camping on Anacapa and Santa Barbara; 30-person limits; no camping on other islands. Permits required for visiting San Miguel. Visitor center in Ventura: exhibits, audiovisual programs. Skiffs or rafts needed for landing on islands.

DAVID MUENCH

KINGS CANYON NATIONAL PARK, CALIFORNIA

28 Lava Beds N.M.
P.O. Box 867
Tulelake, CA 96134
(916) 667-2282

Cave exploration in rugged landscape of cinder cones and lava tubes; prehistoric Indian glyphs. Bird watching in spring and fall.

46,821 acres. Visitor center at HQ: interpretive talks, campfire programs. Notify park ranger before exploring unlisted caves. 41 campsites.

29 Los Padres N.F.
42 Aero Camino
Goleta, CA 93117
(805) 968-1578

Varied landscape with elevations ranging from sea level to 9,000 feet; semidesert areas; stands of pine and oak. Endangered California condors. San Rafael and Ventana Wilderness Areas.

1,752,583 acres. Oct. 15–Apr. 15 best time. Some areas closed during dry season because of fire hazard. Entry permits required for wilderness areas and for camping outside designated areas; reservations required for White Oaks and Sage Hill camping areas. Information at ranger stations in Frazier Park, King City, Ojai, Santa Barbara, and Santa Maria. 1,413 campsites. Food and lodging nearby.

30 Lower Klamath N.W.R.
Route 1, Box 74
Tulelake, CA 96134
(916) 667-2231

Nation's first waterfowl refuge, established by President Theodore Roosevelt in 1908. Marsh, open water, grassy uplands, and croplands attracting huge migrations of marsh birds and waterfowl.

51,713 acres, part in OR. Open dawn to dusk. Food and lodging nearby.

31 Mendocino N.F.
420 E. Laurel St.
Willows, CA 95988
(916) 934-3316

Working lumber forest of pine, fir, and cedar. Excellent salmon and steelhead fishing in Eel River. Yolla Bolly-Middle Eel Wilderness. Water sports.

883,405 acres. May–Oct. best time. Wilderness permits required. Information at ranger stations in Corning, Covelo, Stonyford, and Upper Lake. 477 campsites. Food and lodging nearby.

32 Merced N.W.R.
P.O. Box 2176
Los Banos, CA 93635
(209) 826-3508

Wild millet and other crops attracting wintering Ross' geese, cranes, and shorebirds; also sanctuary for endangered Aleutian Canada geese.

2,562 acres. Open during daylight hours; entry restricted during hunting season. Early spring, fall, winter best times. Food and lodging nearby.

33 Modoc N.F.
441 N. Main St.
Alturas, CA 96101
(916) 233-5811

Timbered plateaus, lush meadows, open rangeland, rough obsidian mountains, lava caves, and craters. Migratory bird refuge. South Warner Wilderness.

1,654,032 acres. Aug. best time. Reservations accepted for Stough Reservoir. Information at ranger stations in Adin, Canby, Cedarville, and Tulelake. 266 campsites, most open May–Sept.

34 Modoc N.W.R.
P.O. Box 1610
Alturas, CA 96101
(916) 233-3572

Some two dozen lakes and ponds flecked with nearly 200 small islands. Canada geese, several duck species, greater sandhill cranes, and pelicans from late spring to early autumn.

6,283 acres. Open sunrise to sunset; Dorris Reservoir unit closed to public during waterfowl hunting season. Apr.–May, Aug.–Sept. best times. Food and lodging nearby.

35 Mono Lake
Bureau of Land
   Management
800 Truxton Ave.
Rm. 302
Bakersfield, CA
93301
(805) 861-4191

Saline lake surrounded by volcanic cones, lava flows, and tufa towers—white spires of calcium carbonate. Many thousands of nesting California gulls and other migrating birds feed here on brine shrimp and brine flies.

20,000 acres. Summer, fall best times. Information at Lee Vining and at BLM's Bishop Resource Area Office, 873 N. Main, Bishop, CA 93514 (619-872-4881). Primitive camping. Food and lodging nearby.

36 Muir Woods N.M.
Mill Valley, CA
94941
(415) 388-2595

Virgin stand of coast redwoods north of San Francisco; named for John Muir, Scottish-born naturalist, author, founder of Sierra Club in 1892.

554 acres. Open 8 a.m. to sunset. Interpretive talks by advance arrangement. Food services; tour bus from San Francisco. Food and lodging nearby.

37 Pacific Crest N.S.T.
U. S. Forest Service
630 Sansome St.
San Francisco, CA
94111
(415) 556-6983

Running through Washington, Oregon, and California, the trail follows the ridges of the Sierra Nevada and the Cascade Range from the Canadian to the Mexican border. Popular for day hikes and short camping trips; hiking the entire trail takes 5 months.

2,600 miles. May–Oct. best time; year round at lower elevations in CA. Some permits required; check with Forest Service. Primitive camping. For information about trail in OR and WA, write or call Forest Service, 319 S.W. Pine St., Box 3623, Portland, OR 97208; (503) 221-3644.

38 **Pinnacles N.M.**
Paicines, CA 95043
(408) 389-4578

Created by volcanic eruptions 23 million years ago, 1,000-foot-high rock formations soar above trails and caves. Wildlife watching.

16,222 acres. Spring best time. Entrance fee. Information at HQ and Bear Gulch Visitor Center in east district; Chaparral Ranger Station in west; evening talks on spring and winter weekends; museum. 24 campsites; group camping forbidden.

39 **Plumas N.F.**
159 Lawrence St.
Quincy, CA 95971
(916) 283-2050

Feather River country of steep mountains, deep canyons, scenic valleys, and jewel-like lakes. Middle fork of Feather designated a wild and scenic river; 640-foot Feather Falls. Includes section of Pacific Crest N.S.T.

1,153,706 acres. May–Oct. best time. Information at ranger stations in Blairsden, Challenge, Greenville, Milford, Oroville, and Quincy. 1,375 campsites, most open May–Oct.; food services. Food and lodging nearby.

40 **Point Reyes N.S.**
Point Reyes, CA 94956
(415) 663-1092

Peninsula 35 miles north of San Francisco, with long beaches, historic lighthouse, meadows, oak and fir forests. Diverse birdlife; sea lions.

70,000 acres. Reservations from Bear Valley Visitor Center. Information center at seashore HQ. 12 campsites, permits required. Most beaches too dangerous for swimming and surfing. Pets on leash permitted on a few beaches. Food and lodging nearby.

41 **Redwood N.P.**
1111 Second St.
Crescent City, CA 95531
(707) 464-6101

Ribbon of Pacific coastline boasts world's tallest trees, ancient coast redwoods soaring as high as 367 feet. Bird and elk watching; wild flowers.

106,000 acres. Summer best time. Entrance fee; backcountry permits required. Information at NPS offices in Crescent City, Hiouchi, and Orick. Camping in adjacent state parks and forests. Tall Trees shuttle bus in summer. Food and lodging nearby.

42 **Rogue River N.F.** *see* Oregon

43 **Sacramento N.W.R.**
Route 1, Box 311
Willows, CA 95988
(916) 934-2801

Pools and seasonally flooded marshes provide feeding and resting areas during winter for huge flocks of geese, ducks, and other migratory birds.

10,776 acres. Open dawn to dusk. Oct.–Jan. best time. Photo blinds available; special use permits required. Food and lodging nearby.

44 Salinas River W.M.A.
P.O. Box 524
Newark, CA 94560
(415) 792-0222

Estuary at mouth of Salinas River harbors masses of wading birds, waterfowl, pelicans, gulls, and terns. Endangered brown pelicans feed and rest here. Endangered Smith's blue butterflies lay eggs in wild buckwheat on dunes.

518 acres. Open dawn to dusk. Fall, winter, spring best times. Information at San Francisco Bay N.W.R. Food and lodging nearby.

45 Salton Sea N.W.R.
P.O. Box 247
Calipatria, CA 92233
(714) 348-2323

Desert basin, mostly submerged under Salton Sea. Huge gatherings of waterfowl, wading birds, and shorebirds.

35,484 acres. Open dawn to dusk. Sept., Jan.–Mar. best times. Limited permits for hunting waterfowl. Advance notice required for guided group tours. Food and lodging nearby.

46 San Bernardino N.F.
144 N. Mountain View Ave.
San Bernardino, CA 92408
(714) 383-5588

Natural recreation area between the Mohave and Colorado Deserts. Lake Arrowhead; section of San Andreas Fault; 3 wilderness areas.

657,938 acres. Fire closure in fall. Permits required for wilderness; reservations required for groups in some areas. Information at ranger stations in Fawnskin, Fontana, Idyllwild, Mentone, and Rimforest. 973 campsites, most open May–Sept./Oct., some year round.

47 San Francisco Bay N.W.R.
P.O. Box 524
Newark, CA 94560
(415) 792-0222

Bayside salt marshes, mud flats, and salt ponds with large numbers of wading birds and shorebirds as well as white-tailed kites and harbor seals.

16,235 acres. Open dawn to dusk. Fall, winter, spring best times. Visitor center near Dumbarton Bridge Toll Plaza: bay wildlife exhibits. Environmental education center for school classes and groups by reservation only; call (415) 262-5513. Food and lodging nearby.

48 San Luis N.W.R.
P.O. Box 2176
Los Banos, CA 93635
(209) 826-3508

Grassland and marsh drawing great gatherings of waterfowl and shorebirds; also a sizable herd of rare tule elk. Vernal pools with spring flower displays.

7,430 acres. Open sunrise until 2 hours after sunset. Early spring, fall, winter best times. Food and lodging nearby; reservations suggested for winter weekends.

REDWOOD NATIONAL PARK, CALIFORNIA

49 San Pablo Bay N.W.R.
P.O. Box 524
Newark, CA 94560
(415) 792-0222

Marsh and open water, chiefly a feeding and resting site for canvasback ducks; also clapper rails, shorebirds, and harvest mice.

12,000 acres. Open dawn to dusk. Winter best time. Groups should notify refuge office in advance. Information at San Francisco Bay N.W.R. Food and lodging nearby.

50 Santa Monica Mountains N.R.A.
22900 Ventura Blvd.
Suite 140
Woodland Hills, CA 91364
(213) 888-3770

Sandy beaches, rolling hills, canyons; oak groves, meadows; waterfalls, valleys, lagoons. Preserves California's Mediterranean ecosystem and various historical and cultural features of region. Surfing; skin diving; whale watching.

150,000 acres. Open daylight hours. Winter, spring best times. Entrance fee for day use of state parks within N.R.A. 100 campsites in state parks. Tours, hikes, special events regularly scheduled. Food and lodging nearby.

51 Sequoia N.F.
900 W. Grand Ave.
Porterville, CA 93257
(209) 784-1500

Groves of giant sequoias, including largest tree in national forest system. Caves, domes, monoliths; mountain lakes and streams. Golden Trout and Dome Land Wilderness Areas; High Sierra Primitive Area. Winter sports.

1,116,000 acres. June–Sept. best time. Permits required for wilderness use and for boating or rafting on Kern River. Information at ranger stations in Bakersfield, Hot Springs, Kernville, and Clingans Junction. 1,070 campsites. Food and lodging nearby.

52 Sequoia N.P.
Three Rivers, CA 93271
(209) 565-3341

Famous for its groves of giant sequoias. 14,494-foot Mount Whitney, highest peak in U. S. outside Alaska, straddles the park's border with Inyo N.F.

403,023 acres. Entrance fee; permits required for wilderness use; reservations required at Lodgepole campground Memorial Day to Labor Day. Park HQ and visitor center: exhibits, campfire programs. 246 rooms; 636 campsites; food services. Caution advised near rivers.

53 Shasta-Trinity N.F.
2400 Washington
  Ave.
Redding, CA 96001
(916) 246-5222

Rolling plateaus, deep canyons, oak woodlands, and granite peaks; Mount Shasta and 5 glaciers; Salmon-Trinity Alps Primitive Area and Yolla Bolly-Middle Eel Wilderness Area.

2,174,013 acres. Aug. best time to climb Mt. Shasta. Reservations accepted for several campgrounds. For taped recreation message, call (916) 246-5338. 1,573 campsites, 4 group campgrounds, some open year round. Food and lodging nearby.

54 Sierra N.F.
1130 O St.
Rm. 3017
Fresno, CA 93721
(209) 487-5155

Wilderness areas and developed recreation sites. Sequoia groves; snowcapped peaks; lakes, rivers, and waterfalls. Sections of Pacific Crest and John Muir trails. Winter sports, including snowshoeing.

1,303,037 acres. Permits required for backcountry use; reservations required for Bass Lake campground. Information at ranger stations in Mariposa, North Fork, Oakhurst, Shaver Lake, and Trimmer Route. 14 resorts; 1,500 campsites; food services. Food and lodging nearby.

55 Siskiyou N.F.

see Oregon

56 Six Rivers N.F.
507 F St.
Eureka, CA 95501
(707) 442-1721

Rugged backcountry covered with Douglas fir. Wildlife includes endangered peregrine falcons and bald eagles. 6 major rivers offer excellent steelhead and salmon fishing; water sports and float trips. Brilliant autumn foliage.

980,501 acres. Most off-highway areas closed in winter. Information at ranger stations in Gasquet, Mad River, Orleans, and Willow Creek. Rooms; 395 campsites. Food and lodging nearby.

57 Soda Lake
Bureau of Land
  Management
800 Truxtun Ave.
Rm. 302
Bakersfield, CA
93301
(805) 861-4191

Last natural alkaline marsh remaining in California. In flat valley between Temblor and Caliente Mountains, lake attracts 13 birds of prey species, many shorebirds and water birds, including 5,000–6,000 sandhill cranes; also bluntnosed leopard lizards, San Joaquin kit foxes, and other wildlife species.

3,000 acres. Fall, winter best times. Information at BLM's Caliente Resource Area Office, 520 Butte St., Bakersfield, CA 93305 (805-861-4236). Primitive camping.

58 **Stanislaus N.F.**
19777 Greenley Rd.
Sonora, CA 95370
(209) 532-3671

Timber and alpine regions, streams and lakes, deep canyons on western slopes of central Sierra. Includes Calaveras Big Tree N.F.; Emigrant and Mokelumne Wilderness Areas; Dodge Ridge and Mount Reba ski areas.

898,322 acres. Spring, summer, fall best times. Backcountry areas open July–early Oct. Reservations accepted at Pinecrest camping area. Information at ranger stations in Hathaway Pines, Groveland, Mi-Wuk Village, and Pinecrest. 1,143 campsites. Food and lodging nearby.

59 **Sutter N.W.R.**
Route 1, Box 311
Willows, CA 95988
(916) 934-2801

Ponds and seasonally flooded marshes provide feeding and resting areas during winter for huge flocks of geese, ducks, and other migratory birds.

2,591 acres. Open dawn to dusk. Oct.–Jan. best time. Refuge commonly flooded part of each winter. Information at Sacramento N.W.R. Food and lodging nearby.

60 **Tahoe N.F.**
Hwy. 49 and Coyote St.
Nevada City, CA 95959
(916) 265-4531

Mixed stands of pine, fir, and hardwood interspersed with barren rock, exposed peaks, and ragged ridges northwest of Lake Tahoe. Winter sports areas, including Squaw Valley.

813,000 acres. Information at ranger stations in Camptonville, Foresthill, Grass Valley, Sierraville, and Truckee. 1,600 campsites. Large areas of privately held land within forest boundary; check map when camping or hunting. Food and lodging nearby.

61 **Toiyabe N.F.**   *see* Nevada

Trinity N.F.   *see* **Shasta-Trinity N.F.**

62 **Tule Lake N.W.R.**
Route 1, Box 74
Tulelake, CA 96134
(916) 667-2231

Marsh areas provide nesting habitat for waterfowl and marsh birds such as egrets, herons, and grebes. Rocky cliffs of the peninsula and Sleepy Ridge are home to hawks, owls, eagles, and falcons.

38,908 acres. Open dawn to dusk. Food and lodging nearby.

63 Whiskeytown-Shasta-Trinity N.R.A.
P.O. Box 188
Whiskeytown, CA 96095
(916) 241-6584

Scuba diving, waterskiing, other water sports in Whiskeytown Lake, formed by dam on Clear Creek; hiking in mountainous backcountry.

42,503 acres. Swimming beaches closed at 11 p.m. Backcountry permits required. Overlook Information Station: interpretive programs, gold panning; campfire program. 193 campsites; food services in summer. Food and lodging nearby.

64 Yosemite N.P.
P.O. Box 577
Yosemite National Park, CA 95389
(209) 372-4461

Beloved by naturalist John Muir, the area within the park lies on the west slope of the Sierra Nevada and includes granite-walled Yosemite Valley and the Grand Canyon of the Tuolumne. Huge granite formations such as Half Dome and El Capitan; rivers with foaming waterfalls; sparkling lakes; groves of giant sequoias; Tuolumne Meadows.

760,917 acres. Mid-May–Sept. best time. Mariposa Grove, Glacier Point and Tioga roads closed by snow mid-Nov.–late May. Entrance fee; backcountry wilderness permits required. Group campsites must be reserved in advance; individual reservations May–Oct. only. Visitor centers: walks, tours, cultural demonstrations, interpretive exhibits, natural history seminars. Ski schools; mountaineering school. Rooms; 1,913 campsites; food services; tour bus. Food and lodging nearby.

WHITE RIVER NATIONAL FOREST, COLORADO

Colorado

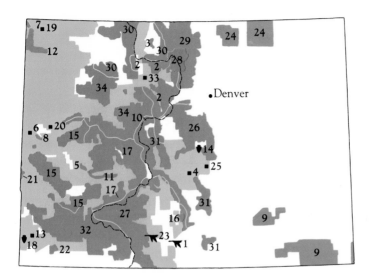

Rocky Mountain National Park sets the high-country tone for federal lands that encompass more than a third of Colorado. Scenic drives take in Pikes Peak, Mount Evans, and other lofty lookouts, but many visitors choose saddle or pack trips through the state's national forests. The ancient cliff dwellings of Mesa Verde and today's renowned ski resorts mark the human presence here.

1 **Alamosa N.W.R.**
Box 1148
Alamosa, CO 81101
(303) 589-4021

High mountain valley along Rio Grande in south-central Colorado. Abundant breeding waterfowl.

10,356 acres. Open weekdays during daylight hours. Apr.–Nov. best time. Information at administrative office, 9383 El Rancho La., Alamosa. Food and lodging nearby.

2 **Arapaho N.F.**
240 W. Prospect
Fort Collins, CO
80526
(303) 482-5155

Land of big mountains and cool, crisp air. Scenic drives over steep roads, including highest paved highway in U. S. 4 wilderness areas with virgin forests, clear lakes, and streams.

1,025,077 acres. July–Oct. best time. Permits required for Indian Peaks Wilderness Area; reservations required for Pickle Gulch camping area. Visitor center at Idaho Springs. 931 campsites. 7 winter sports areas. Food and lodging nearby.

57

3 **Arapaho N.W.R.**
Box 457
Walden, CO 80480
(303) 723-4717

Irrigated and subirrigated meadow and sagebrush uplands bordering Continental Divide. Flocks of birds migrate up and down surrounding slopes.

14,581 acres. Open sunrise to sunset. Spring, fall best times. Food and lodging nearby.

4 **Arkansas River Canyon**
Bureau of Land Management
3080 E. Main St.
P.O. Box 311
Canon City, CO 81212
(303) 275-7578

River fed by streams from mountains of Continental Divide; 86 river miles of narrow canyons and broad valleys. Excellent white water; kayaking championships. Birds and small mammals; grasses, pines, cottonwoods. Gold panning.

57,000 acres. May–Oct. best time. Information at Chamber of Commerce in Canon City. Food and lodging nearby.

5 **Black Canyon of the Gunnison N.M.**
P.O. Box 1648
Montrose, CO 81402
(303) 240-6522

Black Canyon, 2,000 feet deep, is sliced by the Gunnison River and bordered by piñon trees. Wildlife watching.

13,360 acres. Occasionally closed in winter because of heavy snow; South Rim open to traffic all year; North Rim closed to traffic in winter; Rim House open mid-May to Oct. Entrance fee; backcountry permits required. Information at HQ, 2233 E. Main St., Montrose, and at South Rim Visitor Center; interpretive exhibits. 102 campsites. No pets allowed in backcountry. Food and lodging nearby.

6 **Black Ridge Canyons**
Bureau of Land Management
764 Horizon Dr.
Grand Junction, CO 81501
(303) 243-6552

Canyon systems drain off Black Ridge into the Colorado River. Colorful sandstone formations; large cave in Mee Canyon; arches, bridges, windows in Rattlesnake Canyon.

72,440 acres, part in UT. Spring, fall best times. Write or call BLM office in Grand Junction for maps, other information before entering area. Primitive camping. Food and lodging nearby.

7 **Browns Park N.W.R.**
1318 Hwy. 318
Maybell, CO 81640
(303) 365-3513

Wet meadows along banks of Green River in northwest Colorado. Home to mule deer and pronghorns; eagles, hawks, other birds.

13,374 acres. Fall, spring best times. Primitive camping.

8 Colorado N.M.
Fruita, CO 81521
(303) 858-3617

Colorful landscape of fantastic sandstone formations includes 500-foot Independence Monument. Rim Rock Drive affords scenic views into canyons.

20,450 acres. Entrance fee; backcountry permits suggested. Visitor center: exhibits, audiovisual programs. Interpretive talks, campfire programs. 81 campsites. Food and lodging nearby.

9 Comanche N.G.
P.O. Box 127
Springfield, CO 81073
(303) 523-6591

Gently rolling shortgrass and midgrass prairie. Several vertical walled canyons; Indian petroglyphs. 235 species of birds counted here, including geese, ducks, golden eagles, woodpeckers, and shorebirds.

419,000 acres. May–June, Oct.–Nov. best times. Information at Fish and Wildlife Service offices in Springfield and La Junta. Food and lodging nearby.

10 Continental Divide N.S.T.

see Montana

11 Curecanti N.R.A.
P.O. Box 1040
Gunnison, CO 81230
(303) 641-2337

Rough volcanic terrain. Blue Mesa, Morrow Point, and Crystal Lakes, formed by Gunnison River, are excellent for water sports and ice fishing. Winter sports.

42,114 acres. Open 8 a.m.–6 p.m. in summer, intermittently in winter. Spring, summer, fall best times. Reservations required for group camping. Elk Creek Visitor Center: campfire programs, naturalist activities, interpretive exhibits. For information about boat tours, call (303) 641-0403. 335 campsites; food services. Food and lodging nearby.

12 Dinosaur N.M.
P.O. Box 210
Dinosaur, CO 81610
(303) 374-2216

Arid landscape of peaks and eroded canyons cut by Green and Yampa Rivers. Displays of fossils of dinosaurs and ancient reptiles still in rock.

211,141 acres, part in UT. Permits for white-water boating, backcountry hiking; for boating permits, apply between Dec. 1 and Jan. 15 for following season. HQ visitor center in Dinosaur: general orientation; annual Discovery Day program on weekend closest to Aug. 17. Quarry Visitor Center in UT. 134 campsites. Food and lodging nearby.

13 **Dominguez-Escalante Ruins**
Bureau of Land Management
701 Camino del Rio
Durango, CO 81301
(303) 247-4082

Site of Anasazi Indian community in Four Corners area; 11th-century pueblo ruins. 3 miles west of Dolores.

40 acres. Roads not plowed in winter. Information at Heritage Center. Food and lodging nearby.

14 **Florissant Fossil Beds N.M.**
P.O. Box 185
Florissant, CO 80816
(303) 748-3253

Remarkable array of insect, leaf, and seed fossils 35 million years old; also a stand of petrified sequoia stumps.

5,992 acres. Visitor center: interpretive exhibits. Food and lodging nearby.

15 **Grand Mesa-Uncompahgre N.F.**
2250 Hwy. 50
Delta, CO 81416
(303) 874-7691

Grand Mesa has stands of aspen and 250 lakes and reservoirs atop a mesa; rolling terrain in Uncompahgre. Plateaus, jagged peaks, north slopes of San Juan Mountains, canyons, and waterfalls. Winter sports.

1,290,000 acres. Lands End Visitor Center at west end of Rim Drive Rd. 408 campsites, open June–Sept./Oct.; food services. Food and lodging nearby.

16 **Great Sand Dunes N.M.**
Mosca, CO 81146
(303) 378-2312

Dunes created by winds blowing through passes in Sangre de Cristo Mountains. Summer temperatures may reach 140°F at midday.

36,600 acres. Entrance fee; reservations for group camping. Visitor center: exhibits; naturalist activities, June–Aug. 88 campsites. Food nearby.

17 **Gunnison N.F.**
2250 Hwy. 50
Delta, CO 81416
(303) 874-7691

Located in the heart of the Rockies; contains 27 peaks more than 12,000 feet high; buttes, lakes, reservoirs; ghost towns; geologic formations in West Elk Wilderness Area.

1,663,000 acres. Information at ranger stations in Gunnison and Paonia; self-guided auto tour map of ghost towns available from Gunnison Chamber of Commerce. 543 campsites, most open June–Oct., none year round; food services. Food and lodging nearby.

18 Hovenweep N.M.
McElmo Route
Cortez, CO 81321
(303) 529-4465

Ruins of towers, pueblos, and cliff dwellings, built in and around rocky canyons.

785 acres, part in UT. Unimproved road access only. Sept.–Oct. best time. Visitor center. 31 campsites.

19 Irish Canyon
Bureau of Land
Management
455 Emerson St.
Craig, CO 81625
(303) 824-8261

Scenic canyon in easternmost part of Uinta Mountains. Brown, yellow, tan, and white sandstone alternate with deep red to purple quartzite and white limestone. Chukar partridges live amid piñon-juniper woodlands and sagebrush in this semi-arid region.

13,000 acres. Spring, fall best times. 3 campsites. No services for 100 miles.

20 Little Bookcliffs Wild Horse Area
Bureau of Land
Management
764 Horizon Dr.
Grand Junction,
CO 81501
(303) 243-6552

About 100 wild horses roam the steep canyons, sagebrush flats, and piñon-juniper woodlands north of Grand Junction. Best places to view horses: near Indian Park entrance and Monument Rock in summer, Coal and Main Canyons in winter.

27,000 acres. Obtain maps, other information from BLM in Grand Junction before visiting. Primitive camping.

21 Manti-LaSal N.F.

see Utah

22 Mesa Verde N.P.
Mesa Verde
National Park,
CO 81330
(303) 529-4465

Hundreds of ruins of pre-Columbian dwellings, spanning 7 centuries, built on the mesa and in the canyon walls of Mesa Verde—"green table."

52,000 acres. Museum and ruins road open year round except in deep snow; Cliff Palace, Balcony House, and Wetherill Mesa ruins and all concession facilities closed in winter. Hiking permits required; lodging reservations advised. Far View Visitor Center open only in summer; Chapin Mesa Museum open year round; interpretive exhibits, talks; campfire and religious programs. 150 rooms; 477 campsites, some year-round; food services; tour bus.

23 Monte Vista N.W.R.
Box 1148
Alamosa, CO
81101
(303) 589-4021

High mountain valley provides nesting, migration, and wintering habitat for waterfowl; resting and feeding site for greater sandhill cranes and whooping cranes.

14,188 acres. Open daylight hours. Apr.–Nov. best time. Tour route closed during waterfowl hunting season. Information at field subheadquarters, 6120 S. Hwy. 15, Monte Vista, CO. Food and lodging nearby.

GRAND MESA-UNCOMPAHGRE NATIONAL FOREST, COLORADO

33 Upper Colorado River
Bureau of Land
Management
455 Emerson St.
P.O. Box 248
Craig, CO 81624
(303) 824-8261

Excellent opportunities for floating and white-water canoeing between Kremmling and Shoshone; sections for beginners; challenges for experienced boaters. Hikes up side canyons. Hot springs; varied scenery and wildlife.

60 miles. Information at BLM's resource area offices in Kremmling and Glenwood Springs. Primitive camping.

34 White River N.F.
Old Federal Bldg.
P.O. Box 948
Glenwood Springs,
CO 81601
(303) 954-2521

Rocky Mountain high country: 14,000-foot peaks; mixed stands of aspen, cottonwood, spruce, and pine; flower-filled meadows; tundra vegetation; alpine lakes and streams; mineral hot springs. Brilliant fall foliage. Large herds of elk and deer. 7 wilderness areas; 11 ski areas.

1,960,000 acres. Reservations required at 4 group camping areas. Information at ranger stations in Aspen, Carbondale, Dillon, Eagle, Meeker, Minturn, and Rifle. 50 rooms; 1,625 campsites, open end of May–Sept./Nov.; food services; tour bus in summer. Food and lodging nearby.

Connecticut

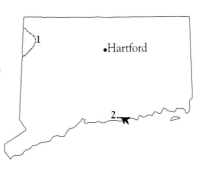

•Hartford

Tidal marshes and cool woodlands are among the varied habitats enjoyed by hikers, birders, and photographers in Salt Meadow wildlife refuge.

1 Appalachian N.S.T.   *see* Maine

2 Salt Meadow N.W.R.
Box 307
Charlestown, RI
02813
(401) 364-3106

Tidal marsh to timberland, where shorebirds, waterfowl, and great numbers of songbirds gather.

183 acres. Open dawn to dusk. Spring, fall best times. Information at Ninigret N.W.R., RI. Food and lodging nearby.

.Dover

Delaware

Migrating shorebirds, waders, and waterfowl vie for visitors' attention at Delaware's national wildlife refuges.

1 Bombay Hook N.W.R.
R.D. 1, Box 147
Smyrna, DE 19977
(302) 653-9345

Marshland resting site for Canada and snow geese; nesting site for mallard, black, gadwall, and wood ducks; abundant shorebirds such as pectoral and least sandpipers, dunlins, and dowitchers.

15,099 acres. Open dawn to dusk. Mid-Oct.–mid-Nov. best time. Food and lodging nearby.

2 Prime Hook N.W.R.
R.D. 1, Box 195
Milton, DE 19968
(302) 684-8419

Marsh and upland along lower Delaware Bay. Large gatherings of snow and Canada geese, black and mallard ducks, other waterfowl; numerous shorebirds; deer; occasional sightings of red and gray foxes, raccoons.

8,926 acres. Open sunrise to sunset. Fall best time. Hunting blinds available for photography by request in off-season. Food and lodging nearby.

District of Columbia

1 Chesapeake and Ohio N.H.P.

see Maryland

2 Rock Creek Park
5000 Glover Rd., N.W.
Washington, D.C. 20015
(202) 426-6832

World's largest natural park in an urban area. Contains historic Pierce Mill, Joaquin Miller Cabin, a nature center, and Carter Barron Amphitheater.

1,754 acres. Open dawn to dusk. Information at nature center. Sports facilities. Food and lodging nearby.

3 **Theodore
   Roosevelt
   Memorial Island**
c/o George
   Washington
   Memorial Pkwy.
Turkey Run Park
McLean, VA 22101
(703) 426-6922

Wooded island sanctuary, a mile long and half a mile wide, in the Potomac River; 2.5 miles of trails; abundant birds and small mammals. Memorial Plaza with statue of Roosevelt by Paul Manship at center of island.

88 acres. Access by footbridge from Virginia shore. Open dawn to dusk. Spring, fall best times. Food and lodging nearby.

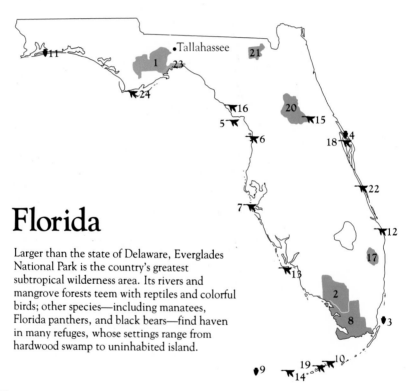

Florida

Larger than the state of Delaware, Everglades National Park is the country's greatest subtropical wilderness area. Its rivers and mangrove forests teem with reptiles and colorful birds; other species—including manatees, Florida panthers, and black bears—find haven in many refuges, whose settings range from hardwood swamp to uninhabited island.

1 **Apalachicola
   N.F.**
227 Bronough St.
Suite 4061
Tallahassee, FL
32301
(904) 681-7265

Hardwood swamps—a forest phenomenon—with species usually found much farther north; also stands of pine, cedar, and cypress; rivers and creeks; natural sinks and bottomland.

558,900 acres. User fee at Silver Lake. Information at ranger stations in Bristol and Crawfordville. 112 campsites, most year-round. Trout Pond Recreation Area for handicapped: fishing, swimming, picnic areas, trails. Food and lodging nearby.

2 Big Cypress National Preserve
P.O. Box 110
Ochopee, FL 33943
(813) 262-1066

Source of fresh water for adjacent Everglades N.P. Important habitat of subtropical plants and wildlife. Ancestral home of Seminole and Miccosukee Indians.

570,000 acres. Permits required for off-road vehicles. Information at Oasis Ranger Station. 75 campsites; food services. Food and lodging nearby.

3 Biscayne N.P.
P.O. Box 1369
Homestead, FL 33030
(305) 247-7275

Mostly water and reef with significant examples of living coral. 45 keys forming a chain from north to south. Snorkeling, scuba diving; bird watching.

175,000 acres. Winter best time. Backcountry permits obtainable from park rangers. Information at park HQ on Convoy Point and ranger station on Elliott Key; interpretive exhibits. 35 campsites. Fresh water available only at Elliott Key Harbor. Food and lodging nearby.

4 Canaveral N.S.
P.O. Box 6447
Titusville, FL 32782-6447
(305) 867-4675

Encompasses lagoons and the only undeveloped stretch of barrier island on Florida's east coast. Many species of birds and other wildlife. Turtle Mound, pre-Hispanic Indian shell midden. Shelling and surfing.

57,627 acres. Open 6:30 a.m. to dusk; may be closed for short periods during NASA space shuttle operations. Winter best time for birds; summer for recreation. Information at seashore HQ and Apollo Visitor Contact Station. Primitive camping in Apollo district, permits required. Food and lodging nearby.

5 Cedar Keys N.W.R.
Route 2, Box 44
Homosassa, FL 32646
(904) 382-2201

9 barrier islands about 4 miles off west-central Florida; large groups of nesting egrets, herons, brown pelicans, and other water birds; also numerous cottonmouth moccasins.

725 acres. Access by boat. Open weekdays during daylight hours; access restricted Feb.–July. Spring, fall best times. Information at Chassahowitzka N.W.R. Food and lodging nearby.

6 Chassahowitzka N.W.R.
Route 2, Box 44
Homosassa, FL 32646
(904) 382-2201

Comprises estuaries, salt marshes, shallow bays, and hardwood swampland; tidal streams and mud bars filled with wading birds at low tide. Thousands of nesting herons and egrets and wintering waterfowl.

30,500 acres. Access by boat. Open weekdays 7:30 a.m.–4:00 p.m. Spring, fall best times. Food and lodging nearby.

LOXAHATCHEE NATIONAL WILDLIFE REFUGE, FLORIDA

7 Egmont Key N.W.R.
1 Wildlife Dr.
Sanibel, FL 33957
(813) 472-1100

Coastal island where sabel palms and wild oats grow. Rich in military history from Civil War through World War II; extensive use during Spanish-American War.

325 acres. Access by boat. Open sunrise to sunset. Oct.–May best time. Information at Chassahowitzka N.W.R. Food and lodging nearby.

8 Everglades N.P.
P.O. Box 279
Homestead, FL 33030
(305) 247-6211

Largest subtropical wilderness in U.S. Open prairies, mangrove forests, cypress swamps support rare birds such as ospreys and eagles. Swimming discouraged; shelling prohibited.

1,400,533 acres. Winter best time. Entrance fee; reservations for group camping. Visitor centers at park entrance, Royal Palm, Flamingo, and Everglades City; interpretive talks, exhibits. 20 cottages; 120 rooms; 344 campsites; food services in winter; tour bus in dry season. Food and lodging nearby.

9 Fort Jefferson N.M.
c/o Everglades N.P.
Box 279
Homestead, FL 33030
(305) 247-6211

Fort Jefferson, largest of the 19th-century coastal forts, is the central feature of the 7 Dry Tortugas Islands and surrounding shoals and waters. Colorful birds and fishes abound. Snorkeling, scuba diving.

64,657 acres. Access by boat or seaplane. Open sunrise to sunset. Bush Key closed to public Apr.–Sept. 10 campsites. All food, water, and supplies must be brought from mainland. Ask Chamber of Commerce in Marathon, Key West, or Naples about charter boats and air taxis.

10 Great White Heron N.W.R.
Box 510
Big Pine Key, FL 33043
(305) 872-2239

Mangrove islands attracting great white herons, white crowned pigeons, and migratory birds.

6,202 acres. Open dawn to dusk. Fall, winter, spring best times. Information at National Key Deer N.W.R. Food and lodging nearby.

11 Gulf Islands N.S.
P.O. Box 100
Gulf Breeze, FL 32561
(904) 932-5302

Historic forts and batteries on offshore islands and a mainland area; portion of historic Naval Live Oaks Reservation. White sand beaches. Scuba diving near Pensacola.

65,817 acres. Open year round, except Santa Rosa and the Pensacola forts; guarded beaches closed Sept.–May. Entrance fee. Interpretive exhibits, programs. 165 campsites; food services. Food and lodging nearby.

12 Hobe Sound N.W.R.
P.O. Box 645
Hobe Sound, FL
33455
(305) 546-6141

Barrier beach and dunes along Intracoastal Waterway; nesting site for loggerhead, leatherback, and green sea turtles; also manatees and numerous waders and shorebirds.

965 acres. Open daylight hours. Fall, winter, spring best times. Food and lodging nearby.

13 J. N. "Ding" Darling N.W.R.
1 Wildlife Dr.
Sanibel, FL 33957
(813) 472-1100

Mangrove and subtropical vegetation of Sanibel Island off west-central Florida. Numerous wading birds, including roseate spoonbills, herons, and egrets; also alligators, otters, and occasional sea turtles.

5,014 acres. Open dawn to dusk. Food and lodging nearby.

14 Key West N.W.R.
Box 510
Big Pine Key, FL
33043
(305) 872-2239

Mangrove islands, habitat of terns, frigate birds, and ospreys.

2,019 acres. Open dawn to dusk. Fall, winter, spring best times. Information at National Key Deer N.W.R. Food and lodging in Key West.

15 Lake Woodruff N.W.R.
Box 488
DeLeon Springs, FL
32028
(904) 985-4673

Freshwater marsh bounded by pinelands and hardwood swamp; home to wildlife such as eagles, ospreys, marsh birds, and alligators.

18,400 acres. Open dawn to dusk. Nov.–Apr. best time. Food and lodging nearby.

16 Lower Suwannee N.W.R.
Route 2, Box 44
Homosassa, FL
32646
(904) 628-2201

Diversified habitats composed of floodplain hardwoods, upland pines, and freshwater and saltwater marshes. More than 250 bird species; numerous alligators and feral hogs.

10,500 acres. Open daylight hours. Spring, summer, fall best times. Information at Chassahowitzka N.W.R. Food and lodging nearby.

17 Loxahatchee N.W.R.
Route 1, Box 278
Boynton Beach, FL
33437
(305) 732-3684

Marshland and cypress swamp bordered by levees; home to rare Everglade kites, limpkins, and Florida sandhill cranes.

145,636 acres. Open dawn to dusk. Late fall, winter, spring best times. Information at wildlife interpretive center, HQ recreation area. Food services. Food and lodging nearby.

18 Merritt Island N.W.R.
Box 6504
Titusville, FL
32783-6504
(305) 867-4820

Sanctuary for endangered birds such as southern bald eagles, peregrine falcons, and dusky seaside sparrows; also robins, tree swallows, and other more common birds.

139,305 acres. Open dawn to dusk. Sept.–May best time. Food and lodging nearby.

19 National Key Deer Refuge
P.O. Box 510
Big Pine Key, FL
33043
(305) 872-2239

Mangrove islands and pine-palm habitat of Florida Keys, home to rare Florida Key deer; also alligators, frigate birds, and other rare wildlife.

5,444 acres. Open dawn to dusk. Fall, winter, spring best times. Food and lodging nearby.

20 Ocala N.F.
227 Bronough St.
Suite 4061
Tallahassee, FL
32301
(904) 681-7265

Unique "wet desert" area of deep, coarse, porous sand covered with sand pine; pools, ponds, lakes, and swamps with subtropical vegetation. Rivers and lakes offer excellent bass fishing. Underwater sports.

381,300 acres. User fee; reservations accepted for group campsites. Information at ranger stations in Eustis and Ocala. 697 campsites, most year-round; food services. Food and lodging nearby.

21 Osceola N.F.
227 Bronough St.
Suite 4061
Tallahassee, FL
32301
(904) 681-7265

Spanish moss hangs from cypress trees beside ponds and in swamps. Stands of pine; orchids, azaleas, and water lilies; natural sinks. Wildlife includes deer and alligators.

157,200 acres. Information at ranger station in Lake City at Rte. 7. 81 campsites. Food and lodging nearby.

22 Pelican Island N.W.R.
Box 6504
Titusville, FL 32783-6504
(305) 867-4820

Islands and surrounding water where pelicans nest and roost; other water birds such as herons, egrets, and ibises.

4,000 acres. Open dawn to dusk. Entry to pelican rookery prohibited. Information at Merritt Island N.W.R. Food and lodging nearby.

23 St. Marks N.W.R.
P.O. Box 68
St. Marks, FL 32355
(904) 925-6121

Refuge along Big Bend of Florida panhandle encompasses freshwater marshes and pools, tidal flats, pine woodland, and Apalachee Bay. 300 species of birds, including wintering flocks of ducks; deer, bears, otters, and alligators. 150-year-old lighthouse; Indian mounds.

65,000 acres. Open dawn to dusk. Fall, winter, spring best times. Reservations for group tours. Historic West Gooseneck seine yard open to public Oct.–Jan. Food and lodging nearby.

24 **St. Vincent N.W.R.**
Box 447
Apalachicola, FL
32320
(904) 653-8808

Coastal barrier island with beaches, dunes, marsh, and woodland; home to wildlife such as pelicans, ospreys, shorebirds, and white-tailed deer.

12,358 acres. Access by boat. Open dawn to dusk. Fall, winter, spring best times. Food and lodging nearby.

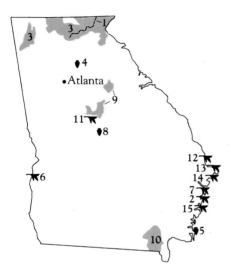

Georgia

Barrier islands provide good resting and feeding areas for hundreds of bird species, some endangered, at Cumberland Island National Seashore and the Georgia Coastal Complex. Shadowy cypress swamps in Okefenokee National Wildlife Refuge, a unique primitive area, shelter one of the world's largest alligator populations.

1 **Appalachian N.S.T.** *see* Maine

2 **Blackbeard**
Island N.W.R.
c/o Georgia Coastal
Complex
Box 8487
Savannah, GA
31402
(912) 944-4415

Barrier island with 9-mile-long beach, freshwater ponds, marshes, and woods. Alligators thrive here, along with thousands of shorebirds, brown pelicans, and black skimmers; loggerhead turtles crawl ashore to lay eggs on summer nights.

5,618 acres. Access by boat; check with complex office. Open dawn to dusk; closed to public during two 6-day hunting periods in fall and winter. Spring, fall, winter best times.

3 Chattahoochee N.F.
601 Broad St., N.E.
Gainesville, GA
30501
(404) 536-0541

Varied terrain of valleys, lakes, streams, piedmont plateau, and mountains. Hardwood forest; spring wild flowers. 2 wilderness areas; Chattooga Wild and Scenic River; 300 miles of trails.

747,094 acres. Visitor center atop Brasstown Bald, Georgia's highest mountain. 521 campsites, most open May–Sept.; food services. Food and lodging nearby.

4 Chattahoochee River N.R.A.
1900 Northridge Rd.
Dunwoody, GA
30338
(404) 394-7912

Series of recreational sites along a 48-mile scenic stretch of the Chattahoochee River, extending into Atlanta.

3,500 acres. Closing hours posted. Visitor information station, Paces Mill unit. Raft rentals, limited food services, and shuttle bus, mid-May–Sept. Food and lodging nearby.

5 Cumberland Island N.S.
P.O. Box 806
St. Marys, GA 31558
(912) 882-4337

Largest of Georgia's Golden Isles, rich in birds and other wildlife. Beaches, dunes, marshes, freshwater lakes, maritime forest.

36,978 acres. Access by boat. Permits required for backcountry; campers must make reservations through seashore HQ; reservations for passenger ferry advised. Information at HQ and Sea Camp Visitor Center. 16 developed campsites; 60-person limit on backcountry camping. Beware of poisonous snakes. Food and lodging nearby.

6 Eufaula N.W.R.

see Alabama

7 Harris Neck N.W.R.
c/o Georgia Coastal Complex
Box 8487
Savannah, GA
31402
(912) 944-4415

Grasslands, marshes, mud flats, and hardwood forest supporting nesting birds such as herons, anhingas, and egrets; also many armadillos and fox squirrels; resident flock of Canada geese.

2,687 acres. Open 8 a.m.–4 p.m. Mon.–Fri. Food and lodging nearby.

8 Ocmulgee N.M.
1207 Emery Hwy.
Macon, GA 31201
(912) 742-0447

Site occupied over a span of 12,000 years, from Paleo-Indians to historic Creeks. Most evident are temple mounds of Mississippian culture and restored earth lodge.

683 acres. Interpretive exhibits and movie; craft demonstrations in summer. Food and lodging nearby.

9 Oconee N.F.
601 Broad St., N.E.
Gainesville, GA
30501
(404) 536-0541

Dense forest of mixed pine and hardwoods growing in red-clay country of rolling piedmont plateau. Reservoirs, streams, and lakes. Ruins of 200-year-old town.

114,270 acres. May–Sept. best time. Information at ranger station in Monticello. 50 campsites; food services. Food and lodging nearby.

10 Okefenokee N.W.R.
Route 2, Box 338
Folkston, GA 31537
(912) 496-3331

One of the largest and most primitive swamps in North America. Cypress-gum swamp, pine forests, freshwater marsh, lakes, and islands. Habitat of white-tailed deer, alligators, bears, otters, wading birds, sandhill cranes, woodpeckers, ospreys, other wildlife.

396,000 acres. Hours vary. Oct.–June best time. Entrance fee charged at northern entrance; permits required for overnight canoe trips. Primitive camping; food services. Guided boat tours available. Food and lodging nearby.

11 Piedmont N.W.R.
Round Oak, GA
31038
(912) 986-5441

Pine and hardwood forest, home to red-cockaded woodpeckers, deer, wild turkeys, and wintering ducks. Diverse wildlife includes 192 bird species, 46 mammal species, and 73 species of reptiles and amphibians.

34,738 acres. Open dawn to dusk. Spring, fall best times. Visitor center; Allison Lake outdoor exhibit. Food and lodging nearby.

12 Savannah N.W.R.
c/o Georgia
    Coastal Complex
Box 8487
Savannah, GA
31402
(912) 944-4415

Tidal creeks and freshwater marsh where flocks of wood ducks and anhingas gather in summer; wading birds such as glossy and white ibises; purple gallinules, popular with bird watchers; alligators. More than half the refuge is hardwood river-bottom swampland, reached only by boat.

26,482 acres, part in SC. Open dawn to dusk; closed during hog hunt in Mar. Summer, winter best times. Food and lodging nearby.

13 Tybee N.W.R.
c/o Georgia
    Coastal Complex
Box 8487
Savannah, GA
31402
(912) 944-4415

Mainly spoil banks where migratory birds rest and feed; among them, brown pelicans, least and royal terns, black skimmers, and laughing gulls.

100 acres. Open dawn to dusk. Spring, fall best times. Difficult access via strong currents downriver from Savannah. Food and lodging nearby.

14 Wassaw Island N.W.R.
c/o Georgia
 Coastal Complex
Box 8487
Savannah, GA
31402
(912) 944-4415

Beaches, dunes, freshwater and saltwater marshes, and timberland; nesting site for loggerhead turtles, ospreys, and alligators; also great numbers of clapper rails and painted buntings.

10,050 acres. Access by boat. Open dawn to dusk; closed to public during 2 deer hunts in fall. Spring, fall best times. Food and lodging nearby.

15 Wolf Island N.W.R.
c/o Georgia
 Coastal Complex
Box 8487
Savannah, GA
31402
(912) 944-4415

Classified as a national wilderness; beach strip, sandbars, and salt marsh; myrtle bushes, cedars; huge gatherings of egrets, herons, brown pelicans, and clapper rails; migrating shorebirds in spring and fall.

5,126 acres. Open dawn to dusk.

Honolulu

Hawaii

Amid tropical lushness, active volcanoes create lava
landscapes at Hawaii Volcanoes National Park.
Colorful cinder cones and blossoming silverswords—
an example of flora native only to Hawaii—brighten
Haleakala's huge crater on the island of Maui.

1 Haleakala N.P.
P.O. Box 357
Makawao, HI 96768
(808) 572-9306

An eroded crater, Haleakala—"house of the sun"—covers
19 square miles on the island of Maui. Unique plants and
animals.

28,655 acres. Spring, fall best times. Permits required for
backcountry camping at Haleakala Crater; reservations
required for 3 crater cabins. Visitor center: exhibits,
interpretive talks. Primitive camping.

2 Hawaii Volcanoes N.P.
Hawaii National
Park, HI 96718
(808) 967-7311

Area of active volcanism on the island of Hawaii. Lush
rain forests provide habitat for iiwis, apapanes, and other
birds native only to Hawaiian Islands.

229,000 acres. Permits required for backcountry use;
reservations advised for Volcano House (hotel) and cabins.
Visitor centers at Kilauea and Wahaula: museums,
interpretive programs. For information about eruptions,
call (808) 967-7977. 35 rooms; 30 campsites; food services.

3 Kilauea Point Administrative Site
Box 87
Kilauea, Kauai, HI
96754
(808) 828-1431

Sheer coastal cliffs on north shore of Kauai are home to
red-footed boobies and wedge-tailed shearwaters; red-tailed
and white-tailed tropic birds and great frigate birds
commonly sighted.

31 acres. Open noon–4 p.m. Sun.–Fri.; closed Sat.
Interpretive center. Food and lodging nearby.

SAWTOOTH NATIONAL FOREST, IDAHO

Idaho

Covering almost two-thirds of the state, Idaho's federal lands enfold vast panoramas of jagged peaks and wilderness areas. Turbulent rivers racing through sheer-sided gorges—including Hells Canyon, the continent's deepest—challenge white-water enthusiasts. Cold streams and alpine lakes teem with trout. Many areas become impenetrable during winter months; summer brings acute forest fire hazards—and pleas for caution to visitors.

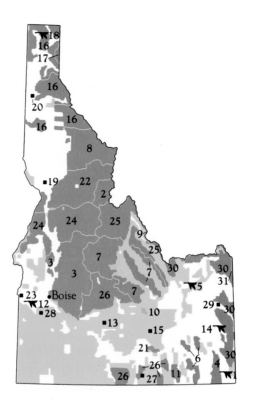

1 Bear Lake N.W.R.
370 Webster
Box 9
Montpelier, ID
83254
(208) 847-1757

Open water and marsh habitat for geese, ducks, and colonial water birds. Greater sandhill cranes nest here; mule deer winter along Merkley Mountain.

17,600 acres. Open daylight hours. Spring, fall best times. Permits required for boating. Food and lodging nearby.

2 Bitterroot N.F.

see Montana

3 Boise N.F.
1750 Front St.
Boise, ID 83702
(208) 334-1516

Stands of ponderosa and lodgepole pines, with some Douglas fir; deep gorges in southern section, high valleys in north; reservoirs and a few natural lakes; several rivers good for rafting; hot springs. Bogus Basin Ski Area.

2,645,927 acres. Reservations accepted for Hot Springs camping area. Information at ranger district offices in Boise, Emmett, Idaho City, Mountain Home; Lowman in summer only. 5 lodges; 822 campsites, open May/June–Sept./Oct.; food services. Food and lodging nearby.

4 **Cache N.F.**   *see* Utah

5 **Camas N.W.R.**
HC 69, Box 1700
Hamer, ID 83425
(208) 662-5423

Marshes, lakes, meadows, and desert. Huge flocks of migratory waterfowl in spring; also waders and shorebirds, mule deer, occasional pronghorns and moose.

10,576 acres. Open dawn to dusk. Spring, fall best times.

   □

6 **Caribou N.F.**
250 S. 4th Ave.
Pocatello, ID 83201
(208) 236-6700

Towering mountain ranges divided by valleys, farms, and ranches. Stands of aspen, pine, and fir on mountains; sagebrush and grasses on lower hills; deer, elk, and moose. Traces of Oregon, California, and Landers wagon trails.

987,187 acres, part in UT and WY. Reservations required for group camping areas. Information at ranger stations in Malad City, Montpelier, Pocatello, and Soda Springs. 210 campsites open late May–Sept. Minnetonka Cave tours June–Aug. Winter sports area. Food and lodging nearby.

7 **Challis N.F.**
Hwy. 93
P.O. Box 404
Challis, ID 83226
(208) 879-2285

Forest includes Borah Peak, Idaho's highest mountain; glistening lakes; fertile valleys; canyons, gorges, hot springs, and marshes; stands of pine and fir.

2,463,604 acres. Information at ranger stations in Challis, Clayton, and Mackay. Ghost town museum in Custer. 276 campsites, open mid-June–mid-Sept. No drinking water in some camping areas. Food and lodging nearby.

8 **Clearwater N.F.**
12730 Hwy. 12
Orofino, ID 83544
(208) 476-4541

Mountainous land cut by deep valleys and densely forested with conifers; clear streams and rivers. Includes part of Selway-Bitterroot Wilderness, noted for large herds of elk. Extensive trail system.

1,688,687 acres. Summer, winter best times. Roads may be closed by snow in winter. Lolo Pass Visitor Station. 12 rooms; 354 campsites, open May/June–Sept./Oct.; food services. No drinking water in some camping areas. Food and lodging nearby.

Coeur d'Alene N.F.   *see* **Idaho Panhandle N.F.**

9 **Continental Divide N.S.T.**   *see* Montana

10 Craters of the Moon N.M.
P.O. Box 29
Arco, ID 83213
(208) 527-3257

Varied volcanic features, including cinder cones, lava flows, and lava tubes.

53,545 acres. Entrance fee; permits required for backcountry. Visitor center: interpretive exhibits, audiovisual programs; naturalist trips in summer. 51 campsites. Food and lodging nearby.

11 Curlew N.G.
Malad Ranger
Office
U.S. Forest Service
Malad, ID 83252
(208) 766-4743

Grassy plains with sagebrush. 129 bird species have been spotted, including birds of prey, grouse, waterfowl, shorebirds. Historic Area: the Oregon Trail Cutoff.

47,626 acres. June–July best time. 10 campsites. Food nearby.

12 Deer Flat N.W.R.
Box 448
Nampa, ID 83651
(208) 467-9278

2 units. Man-made Lowell Lake, where waterfowl such as mallards, pintails, green-winged teal, and Great Basin Canada geese gather in winter; snipes, western sandpipers, other shorebirds in fall; up to 25 bald eagles winter here. Snake River unit, 86 islands where Canada geese nest.

11,585 acres. Open dawn to dusk. Winter best time. Access to nesting islands may be restricted depending on season. Food and lodging nearby.

13 Gooding City of Rocks
Bureau of Land
Management
P.O. Box 2 B
Shoshone, ID 83352
(208) 886-2206

Diversity of landforms: arches, monoliths, and hoodoos— tall columns of earth capped by boulders; eroded channels and plateaus. Sagebrush, grasses; elk, deer, black bears.

19,500 acres. Spring, fall best times. Primitive camping.

14 Grays Lake N.W.R.
Wayan, ID 83285
(208) 574-2178

High plateau with streams and marsh, encircled by national forest and Caribou Mountains; nesting site for whooping and sandhill cranes; breeding waterfowl, including ruddy, goldeneye, and Barrow's ducks and Canada geese; moose, mule deer, coyotes.

18,575 acres. Access limited to protect whooping cranes; viewing platforms open year round. Spring, summer best times.

15 Great Rift
Bureau of Land
Management
P.O. Box 2 B
Shoshone, ID 83352
(208) 886-2206

Rift system, 65 miles long, lying just south of Craters of the Moon N.M.; 800 feet deep in some places. Buttes, lava surfaces, cinder cones. Sparse vegetation; mule deer.

374,000 acres. Spring, fall best times. Primitive camping. Food and lodging nearby.

16 Idaho Panhandle N.F.
(Coeur d'Alene, Kaniksu, St. Joe)
1201 Ironwood Dr.
Coeur d'Alene, ID 83814
(208) 765-7223

Vast area in northern 5 counties of Idaho. Includes Priest Lake, rugged backcountry of Selkirk and Bitterroot Ranges, Coeur d'Alene and St. Joe Rivers; stands of white pine. Includes part of Cabinet Mountains Wilderness.

3,206,338 acres, part in MT and WA. Information at ranger stations in Avery, Bonners Ferry, Coeur d'Alene, Priest Lake, Red Ives, St. Maries, Sandpoint, and Wallace. 481 campsites, open May–Oct. 3 winter sports areas. Food and lodging nearby.

Kaniksu N.F.

see **Idaho Panhandle N.F.**

17 Kootenai N.F.

see Montana

18 Kootenai N.W.R.
Star Route 1, Box 160
Bonners Ferry, ID 83805
(208) 267-3888

Marsh, forest, and upland between Kootenai River and Selkirk Range of the Rocky Mountains. Abundant birdlife, including waterfowl, bald eagles, and ospreys; also deer, muskrats, beavers, moose, elk, and black bears.

2,764 acres. Open dawn to dusk. Spring, fall best times. Food and lodging nearby.

19 Lower Salmon River
Bureau of Land Management
Route 3, Box 181
Cottonwood, ID 83522
(208) 962-3245

4 steep canyons separated by grasslands. White-water rafting for 53 miles.

13,210 acres. July 15–Sept. 15 best time. Permits required for entry into Snake Wild and Scenic River from Lower Salmon. 75 campsites. Food, lodging, and float and jet-boat outfitters nearby.

20 Mineral Ridge
Bureau of Land Management
1808 N. 3rd St.
Coeur d'Alene, ID 83814
(208) 765-7356

Low, forested mountain ridge separating 2 bays of Lake Coeur d'Alene. Winding, 3-mile Mineral Ridge National Recreation Trail. Winter population of 40–70 bald eagles; game fish include kokanee salmon and cutthroat trout.

332 acres. Food and lodging nearby.

21 Minidoka N.W.R.
Route 4, Box 290
Rupert, ID 83350
(208) 436-3598

Sand and sagebrush uplands, grassland, and woods; Snake River and Lake Walcott. More than 200,000 migrating ducks and geese in spring and fall; also great blue herons, double-crested cormorants, snowy egrets; songbirds.

20,721 acres. Open 7 a.m.–10 p.m. Spring, fall best times. Sections where birds are nesting may be closed. Food and lodging nearby.

22 **Nezperce N.F.**
Route 2, Box 475
Grangeville, ID
83530
(208) 983-1950

Rugged land of high peaks and deep canyons, covered with pine, fir, cedar, spruce. Parts of 4 wilderness areas. Wild and Scenic Salmon River and Snake River at edge of forest. Waterskiing; jet-boat trips.

2,218,333 acres. Summer, fall best times. Information at ranger stations in Elk City, Grangeville, Kooskia, Riggins, and White Bird. 143 campsites, most open June/July–Sept./Oct., 1 year round. Food and lodging nearby.

23 **Owyhee River Canyon**

see Oregon

24 **Payette N.F.**
P.O. Box 1026
Forest Service Bldg.
McCall, ID 83638
(208) 634-8151

Rough, remote country with steep mountains and canyons; creeks and lakes; abandoned gold mining camps; stands of large ponderosa pine; part of Frank Church-River of No Return Wilderness.

2,314,037 acres. High backcountry areas accessible July–Oct. only. Information at ranger stations in Council, McCall, New Meadows, and Weiser. 214 campsites, open May–Nov. No drinking water in some camping areas. Winter sports area. Food and lodging nearby.

St. Joe N.F.

see **Idaho Panhandle N.F.**

25 **Salmon N.F.**
Forest Service Bldg.
Hwy. 93 N.
P.O. Box 729
Salmon, ID 83467
(208) 756-2215

Remote forest cut by the Salmon River and its middle fork. Outstanding white-water and fishing area; float and jet-boat trips. Includes parts of historic Lewis and Clark Trail and Frank Church-River of No Return Wilderness.

1,771,180 acres. June–Sept. best time. Information at ranger stations in Leadore, North Fork, and Salmon. 110 campsites, most open June/July–Sept./Oct. No drinking water in some camping areas. Food and lodging nearby.

26 **Sawtooth N.F. and N.R.A.**
1525 Addison Ave.
East
Twin Falls, ID 83301
(208) 733-3698

Pine and fir forest flanked on the east by snowcapped mountains and on the west by jagged pinnacles. Lush valleys; hot springs; sparkling lakes. Surrounds Sun Valley ski resort.

2,122,150 acres, part in UT. Permits required for horses in Sawtooth Wilderness. Visitor centers near Ketchum and at Red Fish Lake. 776 campsites, most open June–Sept./Oct.; food services. Food and lodging nearby.

27 Silent City of Rocks
Bureau of Land Management
Route 3, Box 1
Burley, ID 83318
(208) 678-5514

Granite formations more than 500 feet high, described in one 19th-century account as a "city with tall spires." Mule deer, rabbits, hawks; junipers, flowering cactuses. Remnants of historic Oregon Trail. 4 miles west of Almo.

1,628 acres. Open May–Oct. Spring, summer best times. Food nearby.

28 Snake River Birds of Prey Area
Bureau of Land Management
3948 Development Ave.
Boise, ID 83705
(208) 334-1582

Prairie land and deep canyon 18 miles south of Kuna. Nesting site of one of world's densest populations of birds of prey: golden eagles, prairie falcons, various kinds of hawks and owls. Prey animals include vast numbers of ground squirrels.

482,640 acres. Mid-Mar.–mid-June best time to see birds. Boater registration required. 40 campsites.

29 South Fork of Snake River
Bureau of Land Management
940 Lincoln Rd.
Idaho Falls, ID 83401
(208) 529-1020

40-mile stretch between Palisades Dam and Heise. Canyon walls rise 6,000 feet. Abundant wildlife includes trout, bald eagles, shorebirds, bighorn sheep.

12,000 acres. Spring, summer, fall best times. Information at Targhee N.F. 16 campsites; primitive camping. Food nearby.

30 Targhee N.F.
P.O. Box 208
St. Anthony, ID 83445
(208) 624-3151

Mountain slopes covered with fir, pine, and sagebrush; ranching valleys; large, flat caldera; buttes and canyons; streams, rivers, and lakes; waterfalls. Habitat of trumpeter swans and grizzlies.

1,642,493 acres, part in WY. Summer, winter best times. Reservations required for backcountry use and group camping. Information at ranger stations in Ashton, Driggs, Dubois, Idaho Falls, and Island Park. 899 campsites, open Memorial Day–Labor Day; food services. 3 ski areas. Food and lodging nearby.

31 Yellowstone N.P.

see Wyoming

Illinois

Wildlife refuges spreading along rich bottomlands draw enormous numbers of waterfowl and shorebirds. Several scenic drives afford panoramic bluff-top views of the Mississippi River.

1   **Chautauqua N.W.R.**
Route 2
Havana, IL 62644
(309) 535-2290

Refuge attracts migrating waterfowl in spring and fall, shorebirds in late summer, and bald eagles in winter. 3,500 acres of water; timbered bottomlands; some upland timber on bluff.

4,500 acres. Open daylight hours. Spring, fall best times. Food and lodging nearby.

2   **Crab Orchard N.W.R.**
Box J
Carterville, IL 62918
(618) 997-3344

Wooded upland with 3 large lakes and some 50 ponds; great gatherings of waterfowl, including ducks and Canada geese in fall and winter; also bald eagles; sizable herd of white-tailed deer.

43,022 acres. Half of refuge closed to public. Fall, winter, spring best times. 472 campsites; food services. Food and lodging nearby.

3 **Mark Twain N.W.R.**
311 N. 5th St.
Suite 100
Quincy, IL 62301
(217) 224-8580

9 separate divisions—in Illinois, Iowa, and Missouri—attracting huge flocks of waterfowl on Mississippi flyway; geese and ducks abound seasonally, along with more than 220 other bird species; white-tailed deer, raccoons, and opossums commonly sighted.

23,500 acres, part in IA and MO. Open dawn to dusk. Spring, fall best times. Delair division in Annada, MO, closed to public; most other divisions closed during fall waterfowl migration. Check with HQ about activities. Food and lodging nearby.

4 **Shawnee N.F.**
Hwy. 45 South
Harrisburg, IL 62946
(618) 253-7114

Hills and bottomlands with stands of pine, oak, and hickory interlaced with dogwood and redbud, especially beautiful in spring and fall. Indian mounds.

253,240 acres. Spring, fall best times. Swimming fee. Information at ranger stations in Elizabethtown, Jonesboro, Murphysboro, and Vienna. 473 campsites, most open spring–Dec.; food services in summer. Food nearby.

5 **Upper Mississippi River National Wildlife and Fish Refuge**

see Minnesota

Indiana

Shifting sands of Indiana Dunes National Lakeshore tower a hundred feet or more above Lake Michigan. Set in the southern hills, Hoosier National Forest recalls Indiana's bygone status as one of the world's leading producers of hardwoods.

1 Hoosier N.F.
3527 10th St.
Bedford, IN 47421
(812) 275-5987

Land of undulating hills and sharp ridges; lakes and streams; hardwoods. Picturesque villages and covered bridges draw many artists to the area.

185,000 acres. May for spring blossoms; Oct. for fall foliage. Information at ranger stations in Brownstown and Tell City. 325 campsites, open April/May–Sept./Oct. Food and lodging nearby.

2 Indiana Dunes N.L.
1100 N. Mineral Springs Rd.
Porter, IN 46304
(219) 926-7561

Huge dunes back sandy beaches on south shore of Lake Michigan. Dense forests; bogs and marshes. Cultural arts festival in mid-July.

12,535 acres. Parking fee. Visitor center: interpretive talks, films, programs. Food and lodging nearby.

3 Muscatatuck N.W.R.
Box 351-B
Route 7
Seymour, IN 47274
(812) 522-4352

Diversified habitat of timber, farmland, lakes, marshes, and ponds. Wildlife includes ducks, geese, wild turkeys, and deer.

7,702 acres. Open dawn to dusk. Spring, fall best times. Photo blinds may be reserved. Food and lodging nearby.

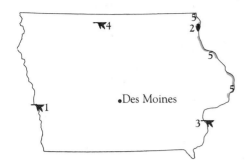

Iowa

Prehistoric burial mounds intrigue visitors to Effigy Mounds National Monument. At the DeSoto refuge, seasonal activities include swimming and boating in summer, bird watching in spring and fall, and ice fishing in winter.

1 DeSoto N.W.R.
Route 1, Box 114
Missouri Valley, IA
51555
(712) 642-4121

Wooded Missouri River bottomlands and open and farmed fields attract huge numbers of migrating mallards and snow geese as well as Canada and white-fronted geese; also wintering bald eagles.

7,823 acres. Open dawn to dusk; recreation area open Apr. 15–Sept. 30. Spring, fall best times. Visitor center: exhibits; views of migrating birds. Photo blinds available by permit. Food and lodging nearby.

2 Effigy Mounds N.M.
P.O. Box K
McGregor, IA 52157
(319) 873-2356

Indian burial mounds, some in the shape of birds and bears, others conical, linear, or compound.

1,475 acres. Apr.–Oct. best time. Visitor center; guided walks Memorial Day–Labor Day. Food and lodging nearby.

3 Mark Twain N.W.R.

see Illinois

4 Union Slough N.W.R.
Route 1, Box 32B
Titonka, IA 50480
(515) 928-2523

Long, narrow refuge with shallow marsh and upland prairie; bromegrass predominant vegetation. Canada geese and 17 duck species migrate through in spring and fall; large numbers of white-tailed deer and ring-necked pheasants.

2,200 acres. Open 7:30 a.m.–4 p.m. weekdays. Spring, fall best times. Nature trail and picnic area open Apr. 15–Sept. 30; Vanishing Prairie Grasslands area open July 15–Sept. 30; auto tour route open periodically. Food and lodging nearby.

5 Upper Mississippi River National Wildlife and Fish Refuge

see Minnesota

Kansas

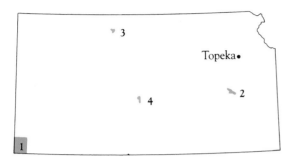

Located in the Central flyway, national wildlife refuges in Kansas shelter large flocks of migrating geese, ducks, and pelicans, and provide nesting areas for Mississippi kites.

1 Cimarron N.G.
737 Villymaca
Elkhart, KS 67950
(316) 697-4621

Rolling southern plains along Cimarron River; Cimarron Cutoff of the Santa Fe Trail. Wildlife includes pronghorns, elk, deer, coyotes, lesser prairie-chickens, wild turkeys, scaled and bobwhite quail.

108,175 acres. May–June, Oct.–Nov. best times.
7 campsites. Food and lodging nearby.

2 Flint Hills N.W.R.
Box 128
Hartford, KS 66854
(316) 392-5553

Grassland, cropland, and riparian habitat within flood pool of John Redmond Dam and reservoir; in spring and fall, waterfowl such as mallards and snow, white-fronted, and Canada geese; large numbers of upland sandpipers; wintering bald eagles.

18,463 acres. Some sections closed in fall; up to 90% of refuge may be flooded at a given time. Spring, fall best times. Primitive camping.

3 Kirwin N.W.R.
Kirwin, KS 67644
(913) 543-6673

Native grasslands fronting lake; trees along shore. Reservoir levels fluctuate greatly. Up to 20,000 Canada geese in late fall and winter, along with mallards, gadwalls, pintails, and teal; prairie dogs, white-tailed deer, wild turkeys.

10,778 acres. Spring, fall best times. 6 campsites. Food and lodging nearby.

Quivira N.W.R.
Box G
Stafford, KS 67578
(316) 486-2393

Sandhills, marshes, and woodlands attract nesting Mississippi kites and migrating white pelicans; also golden and bald eagles; abundant pheasants and bobwhite quail.

21,820 acres. Open dawn to dusk. Spring, fall best times. Food and lodging nearby.

Kentucky

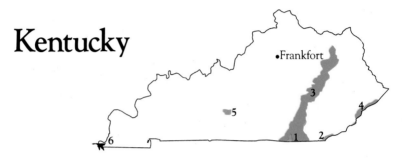

•Frankfort

Underground streams, still at work, have chiseled the world's longest recorded subterranean system—Mammoth Cave. Natural bridges and arches are features of Daniel Boone National Forest.

1 Big South Fork N.R. and N.R.A.

see Tennessee

2 Cumberland Gap N.H.P.
P.O. Box 840
Middlesboro, KY 40965
(606) 248-2817

Memorializes the westward expansion into Kentucky in the late 1700s by Daniel Boone and other pioneers. Miles of scenic trails lead to sites such as Pinnacle Overlook, Hensley Settlement, White Rocks, and Sand Lave.

20,273 acres, part in TN and VA. Spring, summer, fall best times. Permits required for backcountry camping; reservations accepted. Visitor center: interpretive exhibits, campfire programs, craft demonstration. 160 campsites. No trailers or vehicles over 20 ft. allowed on 4-mile drive to Pinnacle Overlook; road closed in bad weather. Food and lodging nearby.

3 **Daniel Boone N.F.**
100 Vaught Rd.
Winchester, KY
40391
(606) 745-3100

Hardwood forest with bluffs and cliffs, delicate waterfalls, large lakes, scenic rivers, natural arches and bridges, and limestone caves. Beautiful autumn colors. Includes Beaver Creek Wilderness, Red River Gorge Geological Area, Natural Arch Scenic Area, Pioneer Weapons Hunting Area, and 254-mile Sheltowee Trace National Recreation Trail.

672,000 acres. Reservations required at Twin Knobs Tent, Trailer, and East Group Use Areas and Craigs Creek Group Use Area. Information at ranger stations in Berea, London, Morehead, Peabody, Somerset, Stanton, and Whitley City. 688 campsites, some open Apr./May–Oct./Nov., some year round.

4 **Jefferson N.F.**

see Virginia

5 **Mammoth Cave N.P.**
Mammoth Cave, KY 42259
(502) 758-2511

World's largest known cave system, extending at least 235 miles. Gypsum and travertine formations.

52,370 acres. Fees for cave tours, Green River boat trip (Apr.–Oct.), and main campground; permits for backcountry camping. Visitor center; guided cave tours; guided nature walks and evening programs in summer. 105 rooms in summer, 58 in off-season; 110 campsites; food services. Food and lodging nearby.

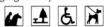

6 **Reelfoot N.W.R.**

see Tennessee

Louisiana

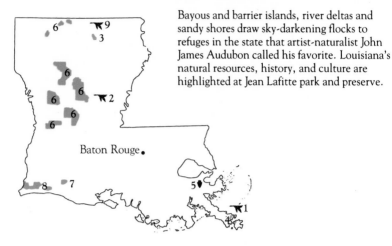

Bayous and barrier islands, river deltas and sandy shores draw sky-darkening flocks to refuges in the state that artist-naturalist John James Audubon called his favorite. Louisiana's natural resources, history, and culture are highlighted at Jean Lafitte park and preserve.

1 **Breton N.W.R.**
Venice, LA 70091
Call New Orleans
Marine Operator
and ask for: (504)
Pilottown 3-3232

Breton and Chandeleur Islands off Mississippi Delta; fine sandy beaches where sea turtles lay their eggs. 20,000 redhead ducks winter here; terns, gulls, and black skimmers nest in summer.

9,000 acres. Access by private boat; motorized land vehicles prohibited. Open dawn to dusk. Information at Delta N.W.R. Primitive camping.

2 **Catahoula N.W.R.**
P.O. Drawer LL
Jena, LA 71342
(318) 992-5261

Bottomland hardwoods of river delta in central Louisiana. Small mammals and deer commonly sighted; huge numbers of small birds such as cardinals, meadowlarks, and wood thrushes; also flocks of waterfowl in winter.

5,308 acres. Open dawn to dusk. Oct.–Jan. best time; refuge normally flooded Mar.–May. Wildlife observation tower. Food and lodging nearby.

3 **D'Arbonne N.W.R.**
Box 3065
Monroe, LA 71210
(318) 325-1735

Bayou D'Arbonne joins many sloughs and backwaters amid hardwood bottomlands and pine forest; home to water birds and upland species such as red-cockaded woodpeckers.

17,421 acres. Open dawn to dusk. Spring, fall best times. Much of refuge may be flooded in winter and spring. Food and lodging nearby.

4 Delta N.W.R.
Venice, LA 70091
Call New Orleans
   Marine Operator
   and ask for: (504)
   Pilottown 3-3232

Marshes, shallow ponds, islands, bayous, and canals along Mississippi Delta. Winter feeding and resting area for 18 duck species, and blue and snow geese; sanctuary for other water birds, shorebirds, white-tailed deer, alligators.

48,800 acres. Access by private boat. Open daily, dawn to dusk, except during waterfowl season. Food and lodging nearby.

5 Jean Lafitte N.H.P. and Preserve
U. S. Customs
   House
423 Canal St.
Room 206
New Orleans, LA
70130
(504) 589-3882

Natural and historical features of the Mississippi Delta preserved in the greater New Orleans area. 3 units, including Barataria, a natural preserve.

8,600 acres. Fall, winter, spring best times. Visitor center, 527 St. Anne St. on Jackson Sq. Food and lodging nearby.

6 Kisatchie N.F.
2500 Shreveport
   Hwy.
Pineville, LA 71360
(318) 473-7160

6 segments with varied terrain: swamps and bayous; creeks, ponds, and lakes; hills and dry ridges. Cypress, oak, magnolia, and pine. Bird watching; waterskiing.

595,000 acres. Spring, fall best times. User fee. Information at ranger stations in Alexandria, Homer, Leesville, Natchitoches, Pollock, and Winnfield. 190 campsites, most open year round. Food and lodging nearby.

7 Lacassine N.W.R.
Route 1, Box 186
Lake Arthur, LA
70549
(318) 774-2750

95 percent of refuge is marsh. Hundreds of thousands of wintering geese and ducks, along with other birds such as herons, egrets, and bitterns; numerous alligators.

31,776 acres. Open Mar. 1–Oct. 15; dawn to dusk. Spring, fall, winter best times. Food and lodging nearby.

8 Sabine N.W.R.
MRH 107
Hackberry, LA
70645
(318) 762-4620

Freshwater and saltwater marshes on Gulf Coast of southwest Louisiana. Flocks of roseate spoonbills, snow geese, and other water birds; also some 9,000 alligators.

142,846 acres. Open dawn to dusk. Late fall best time. Food and lodging nearby.

9 Upper Ouachita N.W.R.
Box 3065
Monroe, LA 71210
(318) 325-1735

Flat hardwood bottomland, bounded on east by Ouachita River; habitat for wintering ducks.

20,905 acres. Open dawn to dusk. Fall, winter, spring best times. Food nearby.

Maine

New England's only national park, Acadia boasts a ruggedly beautiful coastline, serene mountain forests, and glacial lakes. In April and May, visitors to the Moosehorn refuge can watch male woodcocks soaring and plummeting as they stake out their territories.

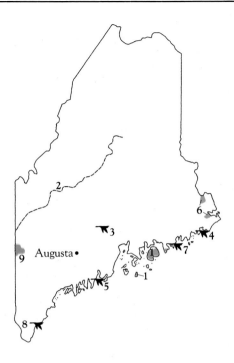

1 Acadia N.P.
Box 177
Bar Harbor, ME
04609
(207) 288-3338

Picturesque rocky coast; forests, lakes, offshore islands, including Mount Desert; Cadillac Mountain.

38,524 acres. Fees for boat cruises. Visitor center: film; naturalist program. Museums on mainland and Little Cranberry Island. 523 campsites. Food and lodging nearby.

2 Appalachian N.S.T.
P.O. Box 236
Harpers Ferry,
WV 25425
(304) 535-2346

From Mount Katahdin the trail follows the Appalachian Mountains through 14 states: Maine, New Hampshire, Vermont, Massachusetts, Connecticut, New York, New Jersey, Pennsylvania, Maryland, West Virginia, Virginia, Tennessee, North Carolina, and Georgia, where it ends on Springer Mountain. Popular for day hikes and short camping trips; hiking the entire trail takes 4 to 5 months.

More than 2,000 miles. Backpacking permits required in Shenandoah N.P. and Great Smoky Mountains N.P. Information from Appalachian Trail Conference, P.O. Box 807, Harpers Ferry, WV 25425. Shelters a day's hike apart along entire trail. Food and lodging nearby.

3 **Carlton Pond Waterfowl Production Area**
Box X
Calais, ME 04619
(207) 454-3521

Wetland area with marsh, bog, and open water habitats. Nesting and migration site for numerous waterfowl species. Located in Troy.

1,068 acres. Open sunrise to sunset. Fall best time. Information at Moosehorn N.W.R. Food and lodging nearby.

4 **Cross Island N.W.R.**
Box X
Calais, ME 04619
(207) 454-3521

Complex of 7 islands in Machias Bay. Nesting site for seabirds, including black guillemots, razor-billed auks, common eiders, and double-crested cormorants.

1,355 acres. Open daylight hours. Spring, summer, fall best times. Visitor permits and reservations required. Information at Moosehorn N.W.R. Food and lodging nearby.

5 **Franklin Island N.W.R.**
Box X
Calais, ME 04619
(207) 454-3521

Partly forested island in Muscongus Bay. Nesting site for seabirds, including common eiders, common terns, Leach's petrels, and herring gulls.

12 acres. Open daylight hours. Fall best time. Visitor permits and reservations required. Information at Moosehorn N.W.R. Food and lodging nearby.

6 **Moosehorn N.W.R.**
Box X
Calais, ME 04619
(207) 454-3521

Diverse region of uplands and woods, with streams, marshes, and lakes, set aside as management area for nesting American woodcocks. Several duck species; bald eagles, ospreys, and shorebirds; also mammals such as bears and porcupines.

22,665 acres. Open daylight hours. Spring, fall best times. Food and lodging nearby.

7 **Petit Manan N.W.R.**
Box X
Calais, ME 04619
(207) 454-3521

Peninsula and offshore islands, home to species such as black ducks, common and arctic terns, black guillemots, and white-tailed deer. Located in towns of Milbridge and Steuben.

2,891 acres. Open daylight hours. Peninsula open Apr. 15–Nov. 15. Spring, summer best times. Information at Moosehorn N.W.R. Food and lodging nearby.

JAMES H. KATZ

ACADIA NATIONAL PARK, MAINE

8 **Rachel Carson**
N.W.R.
Route 2, Box 98
Wells, ME 04090
(207) 646-9226

9 units of salt marsh stretching 45 miles along coast between Kittery and Cape Elizabeth. Waterfowl include Canada geese, teal, black and green-winged ducks.

4,000 acres. Open dawn to dusk. Spring, summer, fall best times. Food and lodging nearby.

9 **White Mountain**
N.F.

see New Hampshire

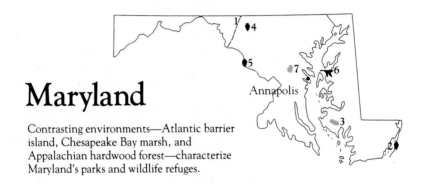

Maryland

Annapolis

Contrasting environments—Atlantic barrier island, Chesapeake Bay marsh, and Appalachian hardwood forest—characterize Maryland's parks and wildlife refuges.

1 **Appalachian N.S.T.**   *see* Maine

2 **Assateague Island**
N.S.
Route 2, Box 294
Berlin, MD 21811
(301) 641-1441 (MD)
or (804) 336-6577
(VA)

37-mile-long Atlantic barrier island includes Virginia's Chincoteague N.W.R., famous for migratory waterfowl. Pony roundup and auction on last Wednesday and Thursday of July.

51,200 acres, part in VA. VA section open 4 a.m.–10 p.m., with shorter hours in winter; MD section 24 hours a day. Spring, fall best times. Permits required for over-sand vehicles, backcountry, and night surf fishing in VA. Visitor centers: interpretive programs in summer. 126 campsites. Food and lodging nearby.

3 **Blackwater**
N.W.R.
Route 1, Box 121
Cambridge, MD 21613
(301) 228-2677

Mainly water and marsh, with some pine and hardwood forest; habitat for white-tailed and sika deer, eagles, and endangered Delmarva fox squirrels; also numerous ducks, geese, marsh and water birds.

14,263 acres. Open daylight hours. Spring, fall best times. Food and lodging nearby.

4 Catoctin Mountain Park
Thurmont, MD
21788
(301) 663-9330

Hardwood forests and streams in foothills of Blue Ridge Mountains offer a variety of recreational activities.

5,769 acres. Permits required for Adirondack (hike-in) shelters and rock climbing. Visitor center: exhibits, campfire programs; wild-flower walks, family walks; moonshining demonstration; photo seminars, other educational programs. 8 cabins; 1 lodge; group campsites for 140 people. Food and lodging nearby.

5 Chesapeake and Ohio Canal N.H.P.
P.O. Box 4
Sharpsburg, MD
21782
(301) 739-4200

Park follows historic 184-mile canal along the Potomac River between Washington, D.C., and Cumberland, Maryland; a towpath runs the entire length of the canal.

20,781 acres, part in DC. Spring, fall best times. Information at Great Falls Tavern and at Georgetown and Hancock Visitor Centers. 31 campsites, accessible on foot or by bicycle. No water at campgrounds Nov.–Apr. Mule-drawn barge rides mid-Apr.–Oct. at Great Falls Tavern and Georgetown Visitor Center. Food and lodging nearby.

6 Eastern Neck N.W.R.
Route 2, Box 225
Rock Hall, MD
21661
(301) 639-7056

Marsh, cropland, and wooded island bounded by Chester River and Chesapeake Bay; autumn and winter gatherings of tundra swans, Canada geese, and a dozen duck species; home to endangered Delmarva fox squirrels.

2,286 acres. Open dawn to dusk. Spring, fall best times. Special deer hunt for wheelchair-bound.

7 Greenbelt Park
6501 Greenbelt Rd.
Greenbelt, MD
20770
(301) 344-3948

Woodland park with marked trails and abundant wildlife. Pine forest harbors raccoons, squirrels, foxes, many birds. Dogwoods, laurels, and azaleas bloom in spring; fall color.

1,167 acres. Open 10 a.m. to dusk. Guided walks, talks, and evening programs. 178 campsites. Food and lodging nearby.

Massachusetts

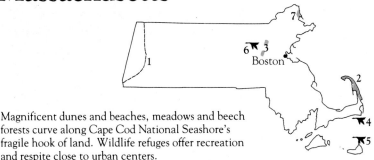

Magnificent dunes and beaches, meadows and beech forests curve along Cape Cod National Seashore's fragile hook of land. Wildlife refuges offer recreation and respite close to urban centers.

1 Appalachian N.S.T.   *see* Maine

2 Cape Cod N.S.
South Wellfleet,
MA 02663
(617) 349-3785

Sand dunes, pinewoods, freshwater ponds, and marshes on outer Cape Cod, site of *Mayflower*'s first landfall in 1620. Historic architecture. Excellent surf fishing; shellfish.

44,596 acres. Open 6 a.m.–midnight. Summer, fall best times. Entrance fee; permits required for over-sand vehicles. Visitor centers at Salt Pond (open mid-Mar.–mid-Jan.) and Province Lands (open mid-Apr.–Dec.). Food and lodging nearby.

3 Great Meadows N.W.R.
Weir Hill Rd.
Sudbury, MA 01776
(617) 443-4661

Marshes and uplands bordering Sudbury and Concord Rivers, only 15 miles from Boston. Nesters such as vireos and warblers; rails and wood ducks; raccoons, minks, and red foxes.

2,878 acres. Open dawn to dusk. Spring, fall best times. Visitor center and wildlife education center. Food and lodging nearby.

4 Monomoy N.W.R.
Northern
  Blvd.
Plum Island
Newburyport, MA
01950
(617) 465-5753

Island with 8 miles of beach, lush vegetation, and freshwater ponds. Great flocks of birds, including golden plovers, least terns, ducks, and geese.

2,700 acres. Access by boat. Open dawn to dusk. Spring, summer, fall best times. Food and lodging nearby.

5 **Nantucket N.W.R.**
Northern Blvd.
Plum Island
Newburyport, MA
01950
(617) 465-5753

Beach along northern tip of Nantucket Island. Great numbers of waterfowl; nesting terns.

40 acres. Access by ferry. Open dawn to dusk. Spring, summer, fall best times. Information at the Trustees of Reservations adjacent to refuge. Food and lodging nearby.

6 **Oxbow N.W.R.**
Weir Hill Rd.
Sudbury, MA 01776
(617) 443-4661

Refuge flecked with ponds fed by winding Nashua River. Black and wood ducks; grouse, pheasants, woodcocks.

662 acres. Open dawn to dusk. Spring best time. Information at Great Meadows N.W.R. Food and lodging nearby.

7 **Parker River N.W.R.**
Northern Blvd.
Plum Island
Newburyport, MA
01950
(617) 465-5753

Plum Island and part of the mainland; sweeps from shore, dunes, and salt marsh to uplands with brush and open fields. Snowy egrets roost in summer; tree swallows gather for migration soon after; huge flocks of ducks and geese.

4,650 acres. Open dawn to dusk; may be closed because of hazardous driving conditions in winter, or when 350-car limit is reached. Spring, summer, fall best times. Photo blinds available. Food and lodging nearby.

Michigan

Great Lakes set the scene for outstanding national sites: Superior's Isle Royale, a water-bound wilderness, and colorful Pictured Rocks; Michigan's Sleeping Bear Dunes, 400 feet high. Where commercial timbering once thrived, national forests now lure canoeists and anglers to scenic waterways; wildlife refuges count hundreds of bird species as full- or part-time inhabitants.

• Lansing

1 Hiawatha N.F.
Forest Service
  Office
2727 N. Lincoln Rd.
Escanaba, MI 49829
(906) 786-4062

2 separate sections of mixed evergreen and hardwood stands bordering 3 Great Lakes—Huron, Superior, and Michigan. Small lakes, quiet rivers, meadows, and marshes. Indian trails and battlefields, old logging camps, picturesque lighthouses.

879,600 acres. May, July–Oct. best times. Visitor center at Ogonotz on U. S. 2. 709 campsites, most open May 15–Oct. No drinking water in Foley Creek camping area. Winter sports area. Food and lodging nearby.

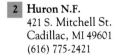

2 Huron N.F.
421 S. Mitchell St.
Cadillac, MI 49601
(616) 775-2421

Rolling hills covered with mixed pine and hardwood and cut by winding, trout-filled Au Sable River; lakes and ponds. Wildlife includes rare Kirtland's warblers.

425,334 acres. Reservations required at Luzerne Trail Camp A. Information at ranger stations in East Tawas, Harrisville, and Mio. 325 campsites, most open April/May–Sept./Nov.; 1 year round. No drinking water in Luzerne Trail Camp A area. 2 winter sports areas.

3 **Isle Royale N.P.**
87 N. Ripley St.
Houghton, MI 49931
(906) 482-3310

Remote wilderness island, largest on Lake Superior, habitat of wolves and moose. NPS facilities for canoeing and nature study.

571,796 acres. Access by boat or floatplane. Open about May 20–Oct. 15. Permits required for boating on Lake Superior. Information at Rock Harbor, Mott Island, and Windigo. 80 rooms; 219 campsites; food services. No roads, vehicles, or telephones available to visitors.

4 **Manistee N.F.**
421 S. Mitchell St.
Cadillac, MI 49601
(616) 775-2421

Replanted stands of hardwoods broken by sand dunes. Good canoeing rivers; wide sandy beaches along Lake Michigan section. Abundant wild flowers and blooming shrubs; fall foliage.

520,969 acres. Group reservations accepted at Bowman Bridge Recreation Area. Information at ranger stations in Baldwin, Cadillac, Manistee, and White Cloud. 433 campsites, open April/May–Sept./Nov. Food and lodging nearby.

5 **Ottawa N.F.**
U. S. 2 East
Ironwood, MI 49938
(906) 932-1330

Wild, thickly forested land; mountains and granite domes; small rivers and lacy waterfalls; pristine lakes; virgin timber. Ghost towns. Winter sports, including ski jumping and snowshoeing.

927,426 acres. Permits required for Sylvania Recreation Area. Visitor center in Watersmeet: films, exhibits, evening programs. Rooms; 515 campsites. No drinking water in some camping areas. Food and lodging nearby.

6 **Pictured Rocks N.L.**
P.O. Box 40
Munising, MI 49862
(906) 387-2607

First national lakeshore, on Lake Superior; scenic region of inland lakes, sparkling waterfalls, deciduous and coniferous forests, colorful sandstone cliffs, sandy beaches. More than 100 inches of snow in winter; winter sports.

71,400 acres. Fees for privately operated summer boat cruises on Lake Superior; backcountry permits required. Visitor centers at Munising Falls and Grand Marais; nature walks and campfire programs in summer. 48 campsites. Food and lodging nearby.

7 Seney N.W.R.
Seney, MI 49883
(906) 586-9851

Within Great Manistique Swamp on Upper Peninsula; 21 ponds sprinkled with timbered nesting islands. American bitterns, marsh hawks, black-billed cuckoos; also Canada geese, sandhill cranes, other birds.

95,455 acres. Open daylight hours. Spring, summer, fall best times. Auto tour route closed Sept. 30–June 15. Visitor center. Food and lodging nearby.

8 Shiawassee N.W.R.
6975 Mower Rd.
Route 1
Saginaw, MI 48601
(517) 777-5930

Floodplain where 5 rivers join to form the Saginaw River 30 miles upstream from Saginaw Bay. Resting site for thousands of tundra swans in spring; also huge flocks of ducks and geese; colonies of great blue and green herons.

8,900 acres. Open daylight hours. Spring, fall best times. Food and lodging nearby.

9 Sleeping Bear Dunes N.L.
400 Main St.
Frankfort, MI 49635
(616) 352-9611

Lake Michigan shoreline and 2 offshore Manitou Islands shelter abundant birds and other wildlife. Beaches and massive sand dunes backed by forests and inland lakes.

70,983 acres. Backcountry camping permits required. Visitor center: interpretive programs. 330 campsites; food services. Food and lodging nearby.

Minnesota

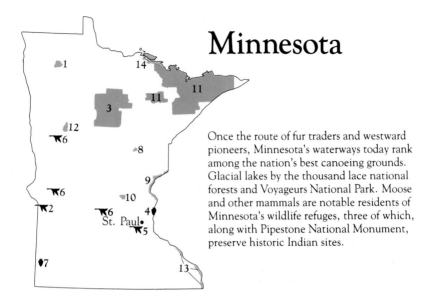

Once the route of fur traders and westward pioneers, Minnesota's waterways today rank among the nation's best canoeing grounds. Glacial lakes by the thousand lace national forests and Voyageurs National Park. Moose and other mammals are notable residents of Minnesota's wildlife refuges, three of which, along with Pipestone National Monument, preserve historic Indian sites.

1 Agassiz N.W.R.
Middle River, MN 56737
(218) 449-4115

Marsh, forest, and brushland, sprinkled with 18 lakes and ponds. 16 duck species; Canada geese and other marsh and water species; moose and deer.

61,449 acres. Open May 1–Sept. 30, dawn to dusk. Spring, fall best times.

2 Big Stone N.W.R.
25 NW 2nd St.
Ortonville, MN 56278
(612) 839-3700

Granite outcrops in canyon carved by glaciers; sections of swamp, marsh, and timber. Large flocks of waterfowl; white-tailed deer, raccoons, and minks.

10,795 acres. Open dawn to dusk. Spring, summer, fall best times. Entry to some areas may be restricted during hunting and nesting season. Food and lodging nearby.

3 Chippewa N.F.
Route 1, Box 25
Cass Lake, MN 56633
(218) 335-2226

Paul Bunyan country of pine woods sprinkled with more than a thousand glacier-formed lakes, including nearby Itasca, headwaters of the Mississippi River. Some virgin timber; berry-picking areas.

661,161 acres. Reservations required for group camping area. Information at ranger stations in Blackduck, Cass Lake, Deer River, Marcell, and Walker. 683 campsites. Food and lodging nearby.

4 Lower St. Croix N.S.R.

see Wisconsin

5 Minnesota Valley N.W.R.
4101 E. 78th St.
Bloomington, MN
55420
(612) 854-5900

Spring-fed marshes and floodplain forest predominate, yet there is enough habitat diversity for more than 325 wildlife species to coexist with man in a major metropolitan area.

4,500 acres. Open daylight hours. Spring, summer, fall best times. Food and lodging nearby.

6 Minnesota Wetlands Complex
Route 1, Box 76
Fergus Falls, MN
56537
(218) 739-2291

Some 700 waterfowl production areas—chiefly prairie wetlands—scattered throughout western Minnesota and ranging in size from 30 to 2,000 acres; managed to preserve nesting areas for ducks and other waterfowl. Part of prairie pothole region, with its thousands of small marshes.

169,000 acres. Open daylight hours. Spring, fall best times. Information at HQ and district offices in Detroit Lakes, Litchfield, and Morris. Not all facilities and activities are available on all waterfowl production areas; check with HQ. Food and lodging nearby.

7 Pipestone N.M.
P.O. Box 727
Pipestone, MN
56164
(507) 825-5463

Quarry surrounded by prairie. Indian ceremonial pipes were made of stone from this quarry for at least 3 centuries. Scenic trail runs past Winnewisa Falls.

283 acres. Spring, fall best times. Visitor and cultural center; carving demonstrations in summer. Food and lodging nearby.

8 Rice Lake N.W.R.
Route 2
McGregor, MN
55760
(218) 768-2402

Glacial moraines thread a vast, level bog. Great numbers of ring-necked ducks, Canada geese, and other waterfowl; nesting bald eagles; also deer, muskrats, and beavers.

18,056 acres. Open dawn to dusk. Spring, summer, fall best times. Food and lodging nearby.

9 St. Croix N.S.R.

see Wisconsin

10 Sherburne N.W.R.
Route 2
Zimmerman, MN
55398
(612) 389-3323

Wetland, forest, and grassland—habitats for waterfowl, bald eagles, sandhill cranes, great egrets, herons, shorebirds, bluebirds, indigo buntings, scarlet tanagers, woodpeckers; also deer, coyotes, foxes, minks, beavers, muskrats.

30,479 acres. Open dawn to dusk. Spring, fall best times. Food and lodging nearby.

11 **Superior N.F.**
P.O. Box 338
Duluth, MN 55801
(218) 727-6692

More than 300,000 acres of clear, cold lakes and streams scattered throughout pine, alder, and birch woods. Expanses of virgin timber; Boundary Waters Canoe Area Wilderness.

2,049,405 acres. Permits required for wilderness area. Voyageur Visitor Center 2 miles east of Ely on Minn. 169; open June 1–Labor Day; exhibits, lectures. 642 campsites, open May/June–Sept./Oct.; food services. Food and lodging nearby.

12 **Tamarac N.W.R.**
Rural Route
Rochert, MN 56578
(218) 847-2641

Marsh and timberland with some two dozen lakes. Wide range of birdlife, including ducks, geese, and bald and golden eagles; also mammals such as deer and bears.

42,725 acres. Open dawn to dusk. Spring, fall best times. Visitor center. Food and lodging nearby.

13 **Upper Mississippi River National Wildlife and Fish Refuge**
51 E. 4th St.
Winona, MN 55987
(507) 452-4232

Longest inland federal refuge, extending 284 miles along Mississippi River from Wabash, Minnesota, to Rock Island, Illinois. Bottomland forests, islands, marshes, sloughs, and backwater lakes. Important resting and feeding area for migratory waterfowl. Bottomlands harbor marsh birds and shorebirds. Mammals include muskrats, minks, beavers, raccoons, otters, skunks, weasels, foxes, white-tailed deer.

195,000 acres, part in IL, IA, and WI. Spring, fall best times. Information at district offices in Winona, MN, Lansing, IA, Savanna, IL, and Cassville and LaCrosse, WI. Primitive camping. Not all activities apply to all parts of refuge; check with HQ. Food and lodging nearby.

14 **Voyageurs N.P.**
P.O. Box 50
International Falls, MN 56649
(218) 283-9821

Forested region of large lakes dotted with hundreds of islands; part of historic 3,000-mile route of French Canadian voyageurs; land and waterways carved by glaciers.

217,324 acres. Access in summer by boat or floatplane; in winter by ice road, snowmobile, ski-plane, skis, or snowshoes. May–Oct. best time. Information at park HQ and Kabetogama Lake Visitor Center. Rooms; more than 100 island campsites; food services. Food and lodging nearby.

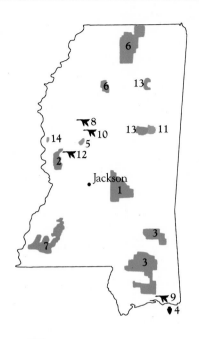

Mississippi

Wildlife and history as well as fine beaches reward vacationers at Gulf Islands National Seashore. Inland, handsome hardwood stands and lazy rivers provide cooling retreats for visitors to the state's national forests.

1 **Bienville N.F.**
Box 30
Forest, MS 39074
(601) 469-3811

Second-growth woodland on coastal plain; yellow pine, oak, poplar, ash, and hickory; stand of virgin loblolly pine. Includes a national recreation trail and Harrell Prairie Hill Botanical Area.

180,000 acres. Spring, early fall best times. User fee. Information at ranger stations in Forest and Raleigh. 48 campsites, open year round. Food and lodging nearby.

2 **Delta N.F.**
Sharkey-Ag Bldg.
402 Hwy. 61 N.
Rolling Fork, MS
39159
(601) 873-6256

Bottomland hardwood forest of oak, sweetgum, sugarberry, ash, water hickory, and cypress. Timberland flooded in winter attracts waterfowl.

59,500 acres. Fall, winter best times. Camping permits required during hunting season. Information at ranger station in Rolling Fork. 87 campsites. Food and lodging nearby.

3 **DeSoto N.F.**
Route 1, Box 62
McHenry, MS 39561
(601) 928-5291

Level to rolling forest scattered in sections throughout southeastern Mississippi; rivers, streams, and small lakes; semitropical vegetation. Tuxachanie Trail; float trips.

500,000 acres. Spring, fall best times. Entrance fee for Turkey Fork Recreation Area. Information at ranger stations in Laurel, McHenry, and Wiggins. 40 campsites, most open Apr.–Sept. or Mar.–Nov., a few year round. Food and lodging nearby.

MISSISSIPPI SANDHILL CRANE NATIONAL WILDLIFE REFUGE, MISSISSIPPI

Missouri

Scenic rivers—including the federally designated Current, Jacks Fork, and Eleven Point—invite relaxing float trips beneath Ozark ridgetops. Of particular note at wildlife refuges: Mingo's ancient swamp and Squaw Creek's large winter population of bald eagles.

Jefferson City•

1 **Mark Twain N.F.**
401 Fairgrounds Rd.
Rolla, MO 65401
(314) 364-4621

13 districts with varied terrain: ridges, hills, and hollows; rock outcrops; valleys; prairies. Pine, oak, dogwood, redbud, and cedar. Working mines. 6 wilderness areas. Float trips.

1,500,000 acres. Open daylight hours. Spring, fall best times. Information at ranger district offices in Ava, Cassville, Doniphan, Fredericktown, Fulton, Houston, Poplar Bluff, Potosi, Rolla, Salem, Van Buren, Willow Springs, and Winona. 675 campsites. Food and lodging nearby.

2 **Mark Twain N.W.R.**

see Illinois

3 **Mingo N.W.R.**
Route 1, Box 103
Puxico, MO 63960
(314) 222-3589

Chiefly swamp, with some farm tracts and upland timbered with hickory and oak. Waterfowl in spring and fall; wintering bald eagles; wild turkeys and deer.

21,676 acres. Sections open year round, dawn to dusk. Fall best time. Food and lodging nearby.

4 **Ozark N.S.R.**
P.O. Box 490
Van Buren, MO 63965
(314) 323-4236

Float trips and water sports on 134 miles of Current and Jacks Fork Rivers. Numerous springs and caves; other natural and cultural resources.

80,788 acres. Apr.–Nov. best time. Reservations for group campsites. Visitor center: interpretive talks; cave tours; craft demonstrations. Rooms; 665 campsites; food services. Food and lodging nearby.

5 **Squaw Creek N.W.R.**
Box 101
Mound City, MO 64470
(816) 442-3187

Marsh, woods, and grassland noted for gatherings of up to 200 bald eagles in winter; hundreds of thousands of waterfowl such as snow and Canada geese, and mallard, shoveler, and pintail ducks; white pelicans in spring and fall.

6,887 acres. Open dawn to dusk. Spring, fall best times. Food and lodging nearby.

6 **Swan Lake N.W.R.**
Box 68
Sumner, MO 64681
(816) 856-3323

Set aside for waterfowl; attracts perhaps 200,000 Canada geese in autumn.

10,670 acres. Open Mar. 1–Oct. 15, dawn to dusk. Spring, fall best times. Food and lodging nearby.

MULE DEER IN GLACIER NATIONAL PARK, MONTANA

Montana

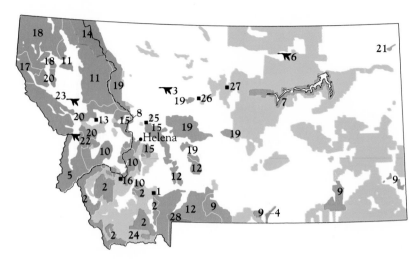

Massive ramparts of the Rockies lend dramatic dimensions to much of the federal domain that takes in almost a third of Montana. Astride the Continental Divide, Glacier National Park—now linked to Canada's Waterton Lakes National Park—is a million-acre wonderland of stark peaks and flower-filled meadows, sparkling lakes, glaciers, and waterfalls. Wildlife abounds here and throughout Montana's federal preserve; big-game hunting is especially popular in national forests also known for their vast wilderness areas.

1 **Bear Trap Canyon**
Bureau of Land
   Management
Ibey Building
P.O. Box 1048
Dillon, MT 59725
(406) 683-2337

Wilderness area on Madison River 30 miles west of Bozeman; 9-mile gorge with 1,500-foot cliffs. Hiking trail parallels river; white water for experienced boaters only.

5,719 acres. Access from north only. Summer, fall best times. Information at BLM offices in Dillon and Butte. BLM Red Mountain Campground 2 miles from north boundary. Food, lodging, and white-water outfitters nearby.

2 **Beaverhead N.F.**
Montana 41 and
   Skiki St.
Dillon, MT 59725
(406) 683-2312

High, rough country of snowcapped mountain ranges separated by lush grazing valleys. Dense stands of spruce, Douglas fir, and lodgepole pine. Historic Indian battlefield.

2,112,000 acres. Visitor center at Big Hole National Battlefield. 100 rooms; 250 campsites, most open late June–mid-Sept.; food services. Food and lodging nearby.

3 **Benton Lake N.W.R.**
Box 450
Black Eagle, MT
59414
(406) 727-7400

Glacial lake subdivided into 6 marsh units bounded by grassland. Great flocks of migrating waterfowl and shorebirds; 20,000 ducks, several thousand Franklin gulls and eared grebes; also Canada geese, avocets, and western phalaropes.

12,383 acres. Open Mar.–Nov., dawn to dusk. Spring, fall best times. Food and lodging nearby.

4 **Bighorn Canyon N.R.A.**
P.O. Box 458
Fort Smith, MT
59035
(406) 666-2412

Reservoir 71 miles long in deep, rugged Bighorn Canyon, adjacent to Crow Indian Reservation. Water sports include ice fishing in winter.

120,158 acres, part in WY. Visitor centers; weekend visitor programs in summer; Yellowtail center closed Oct.–Apr. 125 campsites. Food and lodging nearby.

5 **Bitterroot N.F.**
316 N. 3rd St.
Hamilton, MT
59840
(406) 363-3131

Mountain ranges blanketed with pine, fir, and spruce. Alpine lakes; hot springs. Indian petroglyphs. Includes parts of Selway-Bitterroot, Anaconda-Pintler, and Frank Church-River of No Return Wilderness Areas.

1,578,000 acres, part in ID. 228 campsites, open May/June–Sept./Nov. Food and lodging nearby.

6 **Bowdoin N.W.R.**
Box J
Malta, MT 59538
(406) 654-2863

Water, marsh, and prairie where thousands of water birds nest in spring; ducks, geese, white pelicans, gulls, black terns, Wilson's phalaropes, avocets; habitat for pronghorns and white-tailed deer.

15,437 acres. Open dawn to dusk. Spring, fall best times. Refuge roads and trails sometimes closed by bad weather. Food and lodging nearby.

7 **Charles M. Russell N.W.R.**
Box 110
Lewistown, MT
59457
(406) 538-8707

Region of prairie, woodland, and waterways, home to mammals such as elk, bighorn sheep, mule and white-tailed deer, pronghorns, desert cottontails; owls, mountain plovers; nesting golden eagles in summer.

1,094,000 acres. Spring, summer, fall best times. Primitive camping; camping also in 5 state parks within refuge. Food and lodging nearby.

8 **Continental Divide N.S.T.**
U. S. Forest Service
11177 W. 8th Ave.
Box 25127
Lakewood, CO
80225
(303) 234-4082

Not yet continuous, the trail zigzags across the Continental Divide—shown as a broken black line—in Montana, Idaho, Wyoming, Colorado, and New Mexico; passes through 25 national forests and 3 national parks. Popular for day hikes and short camping trips; hiking the entire trail takes 5 months.

3,100 miles. May–Oct. best time. Information from any local N.F. or N.P. HQ. Primitive camping.

9 **Custer N.F.**
P.O. Box 2556
Billings, MT 59103
(406) 657-6361

Snowcapped granite peaks, timbered slopes, rolling pine hills and grasslands. Beartooth Primitive Area, with 12,000-foot mountains, glaciers, lakes, and waterfalls.

1,186,000 acres, part in SD. Information at ranger stations in Ashland, Camp Crook, Dickinson, Lemmon, Lisbon, Red Lodge, and Watford City. 250 campsites, most open May/June–mid-Sept.; food services. Food and lodging nearby.

10 **Deerlodge N.F.**
Federal Building
Box 400
Butte, MT 59701
(406) 496-3400

Snowcapped mountains, gentle foothills, and lush river valleys straddling the Continental Divide. Wildlife includes pronghorns and mountain goats. Ghost towns.

1,195,754 acres. Information at ranger stations in Butte, Deer Lodge, Philipsburg, and Whitehall. 185 campsites, most open mid-June–mid-Sept. Food and lodging nearby.

11 **Flathead N.F.**
P.O. Box 147
1935 3rd Ave. E.
Kalispell, MT 59901
(406) 755-5401

River valleys, canyons, peaks, glaciers, lakes; larch, pine, and fir; virgin timber; grizzlies, wolves, eagles, and falcons. 3 wilderness areas; wild and scenic rivers.

2,346,000 acres. Hungry Horse Dam Visitor Center. 400 campsites, open June–mid-Sept.

12 **Gallatin N.F.**
Federal Building
Box 130
Bozeman, MT 59715
(406) 587-5271

Rugged peaks and ridges; valleys and canyons; rivers and creeks; waterfalls; wilderness and primitive areas. Site of 1959 earthquake set aside for observation.

1,735,000 acres. Visitor center at Madison Earthquake Area. 1,000 campsites, most open June/July–mid-Sept. 2 winter sports areas. Food and lodging nearby.

CHARLES M. RUSSELL NATIONAL WILDLIFE REFUGE, MONTANA

4 **Nebraska N.F.**
270 Pine St.
Chadron, NE 69337
(308) 432-3367

Pine forest planted amid rolling grassland in sandhills; also naturally forested lands along rugged Pine Ridge Escarpment. Nesting ground of great blue herons and prairie-chickens. Includes Samuel R. McKelvie N.F. and Bessey Nursery.

257,257 acres. May–Sept. best time. Information at ranger stations in Chadron and Halsey. 53 campsites, open May–Sept. Food and lodging nearby.

5 **Oglala N.G.**
270 Pine St.
Chadron, NE 69337
(308) 432-3367

Flat to rolling prairie; "toadstool" formations characteristic of Nebraska Badlands. Fossil area. Rock hunters can find a variety of agates and other rocks.

94,332 acres. Summer best time. Muddy roads in spring. Primitive camping. Food and lodging nearby.

6 **Rainwater Basin W.M.D.**
Box 1786
Kearney, NE 68847
(308) 236-5015

40 waterfowl production areas; prairie grasslands with natural wetlands, important in supporting migrating birds and resident wildlife.

15,000 acres. Spring, fall best times. Food and lodging nearby.

Samuel R. McKelvie N.F.

see **Nebraska N.F.**

7 **Scotts Bluff N.M.**
P.O. Box 427
Gering, NE 69341
(308) 436-4340

800-foot cliff overlooking Oregon Trail; landmark for thousands of pioneers who crossed the Great Plains between 1843 and 1869; wheel ruts still visible.

2,988 acres. Open 8 a.m.–5 p.m. in winter; extended hours in summer. Road to top closed intermittently by snow in winter. Entrance fee. Museum, living history programs. Food and lodging nearby.

8 **Valentine N.W.R.**
c/o Fort Niobrara
N.W.R.
Hidden Timber
Route
Valentine, NE 69201
(402) 376-3789

Meadows, grassland, and sand dunes—sprinkled with lakes and marshes—attract tens of thousands of migrating shorebirds such as dowitchers and Wilson's phalaropes; nesters include avocets, American bitterns, and upland sandpipers.

71,516 acres. Open dawn to dusk. Spring, fall best times. Information at Fort Niobrara N.W.R. Photo blinds available.

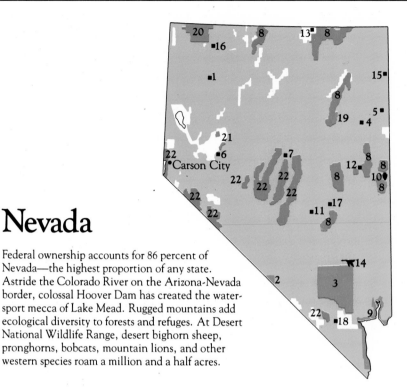

Nevada

Federal ownership accounts for 86 percent of Nevada—the highest proportion of any state. Astride the Colorado River on the Arizona-Nevada border, colossal Hoover Dam has created the water-sport mecca of Lake Mead. Rugged mountains add ecological diversity to forests and refuges. At Desert National Wildlife Range, desert bighorn sheep, pronghorns, bobcats, mountain lions, and other western species roam a million and a half acres.

1 | **Black Rock Desert**
Bureau of Land Management
705 E. 4th St.
Winnemucca, NV 89445
(702) 623-3676

Y-shaped desert area, site of prehistoric lake; explored by John Charles Frémont in 1840s; crossed by historic Applegate-Lassen Trail, route of forty-niners. Wild horses roam the area. Remains of 1860s mining camp.

694,000 acres. Spring, fall best times. Playa section impassable in winter or after rain. Information at Gerlach; inquire there about road conditions, hazards. Primitive camping; good drinking water at Gerlach only. Food and lodging nearby.

2 | **Death Valley N.M.**

see California

3 | **Desert National Wildlife Range**
1500 N. Decatur Blvd.
Las Vegas, NV 89108
(702) 646-3401

Varied country, from scorching desert to snowcapped peaks. Noted for largest known gathering of desert bighorn sheep; golden eagles abundant in spring; sage sparrows, Le Conte's thrashers, and hepatic tanagers also common.

1,500,000 acres. Open 5 a.m.–9 p.m. Spring, fall best times. Primitive camping, June 1–Nov. 10; permits required.

BRISTLECONE PINES IN HUMBOLDT NATIONAL FOREST, NEVADA

4 **Goshute Canyon Natural Area**
Bureau of Land Management
Star Route, Box 1
Ely, NV 89301
(702) 289-4865

Narrow canyon in Cherry Creek Range, 60 miles north of Ely. The creek's Utah cutthroat trout are on Nevada's endangered species list. Sagebrush, bristlecone pines, willows, cottonwoods, and aspens grow here.

7,650 acres. Access by rough dirt roads. May–Oct. best time. Primitive camping. Food and lodging nearby.

5 **Goshute Mountains**
Bureau of Land Management
P.O. Box 831
Elko, NV 89801
(702) 738-4071

Wilderness study area 20 miles southwest of West Wendover. Wild horses; annual birds of prey migration; wintering habitat for bald eagles; mule deer, mountain lions, marmots, songbirds; sagebrush, piñons, limber pines.

125,000 acres. Apr.–Oct. best time. Primitive camping.

6 **Grimes Point Archaeological Area**
Bureau of Land Management
1050 E. William St.
Carson City, NV 89701
(702) 882-1631

Dry, rocky area containing several hundred boulders with petroglyphs; caves and shelters of hunter-gatherers from 5000 B.C. Wildlife includes ravens, rabbits, coyotes, lizards. 10 miles southeast of Fallon.

340 acres. Spring, fall best times. Information at Churchill County Museum in Fallon. Food and lodging nearby.

7 **Hickison Petroglyph Recreation Site**
Bureau of Land Management
P.O. Box 1420
Battle Mountain, NV 89820
(702) 635-5181

Human and animal figures incised in stone, 1000 B.C.– A.D. 1500; site used for ceremonial functions by primitive hunters. Route of Pony Express; abandoned gold and silver mines from 1860s.

40 acres. Open Apr. 1–Nov. 1. Summer best time. 16 campsites. No water available.

8 **Humboldt N.F.**
976 Mountain City Hwy.
Elko, NV 89801
(702) 738-5171

Snowcapped ranges greened by pine and aspen and separated by desert flats. Wheeler Peak with ancient bristlecone pines; Wild Horse Reservoir; lakes and streams. Includes Jarbridge Wilderness.

2,527,929 acres. Visitor center near Wheeler Peak. 300 campsites, most open late May to Oct. Food and lodging nearby.

9 **Lake Mead N.R.A.**
601 Nevada Hwy.
Boulder City, NV 89005
(702) 293-4041

First national recreation area, established in 1936. Reservoirs of Lakes Mead and Mohave on the Colorado River; desert canyons and plateaus. Dam tours; botanical garden; waterskiing.

1,496,601 acres, part in AZ. Late Sept.–late May best time. Alan Bible Visitor Center: interpretive programs. 214 rooms; 1,148 campsites; food services. Hikers should carry enough water; springwater not suitable for drinking. Food and lodging nearby.

10 **Lehman Caves N.M.**
Baker, NV 89311
(702) 234-7331

Gray- and white-marbled caverns beneath flank of 13,000-foot Wheeler Peak; named after pioneer Absalom Lehman.

640 acres. Open 8 a.m.–5 p.m. Tour and guide fees; permits required for cave tours. Visitor center; hourly tours in summer; Oct.–May at 9, 11, 2, and 4. Food services in summer. 4 campgrounds in adjacent Humboldt N.F. Food and lodging nearby.

11 **Lunar Crater Volcanic Field**
Bureau of Land Management
P.O. Box 1420
Battle Mountain, NV 89820
(702) 635-5181

Crater 430 feet deep and 3,800 feet wide; lava flows, cinder cones; Easy Chair Crater, The Wall, Black Rock Lava Flow, other geologic features. Pronghorns, kit foxes, ravens; shrubs, wild flowers. South of Ely.

64,000 acres. Summer best time.

12 **Mount Grafton Wilderness Study Area**
Bureau of Land Management
Star Route 5, Box 1
Ely, NV 89301
(702) 289-4865

Mountains 5,500–10,990 feet high. Bristlecone pines—earth's oldest living things—grow here. Wildlife includes pronghorns, elk, deer, bobcats, mountain lions, blue grouse. 5 miles south of Ely.

73,261 acres. Access by rough dirt roads. July–Sept. best time. Primitive camping.

13 **Owyhee River Canyon**

see Oregon

14 **Pahranagat N.W.R.**
P.O. Box 519
Alamo, NV 89001
(702) 725-3417

Marsh and open water, home to birds such as white-crowned and black-throated sparrows, Bullock's orioles, water pipits, marsh hawks, and green-tailed towhees.

5,380 acres. Spring, fall, winter best times. Primitive camping. Food and lodging nearby.

15 Pilot Peak
Bureau of Land
  Management
P.O. Box 831
Elko, NV 89801
(702) 738-4071

Steep 10,704-foot peak 15 miles north of West Wendover; landmark for early explorers and settlers heading west across barren salt flats. Elk, mule, deer, mountain lions, and pikas live here; also eagles, hawks, songbirds.

19,000 acres. Apr.–June best time. Primitive camping. Food and lodging nearby.

**16 Pine Forest-Blue
    Lake**
Bureau of Land
  Management
705 E. 4th St.
Winnemucca, NV
89445
(702) 623-3676

Semi-arid mountainous region with lake and canyons gouged by a glacier. Coyotes, deer, small mammals, and songbirds; aspen groves and wild flowers. 30 miles southwest of Denio Junction.

16,000 acres. Closed in winter. Summer best time. Primitive camping. No drinking water available. Rough roads; 4-wheel-drive vehicle usually needed.

**17 Railroad Valley
    W.M.A.**
Bureau of Land
  Management
P.O. Box 1420
Battle Mountain,
NV 89820
(702) 635-5181

Marshes and ponds attracting nesting and migratory waterfowl such as geese and tundra swans; also herons, egrets, swallows, and flycatchers; more than 100 bird species counted; habitats for various fishes and mammals. Between Ely and Tonopah.

14,720 acres. Spring best time.

**18 Red Rock Canyon
    Recreation Lands**
Bureau of Land
  Management
P.O. Box 7384
Las Vegas, NV 89125
(702) 363-1921

Red-and-yellow sandstone cliffs dominate landscape. Desert bighorn sheep frequent springs and pools in water-carved canyons and on top of cliffs. Rock art, roasting pits, and temporary campsites left by ancient Indian visitors.

62,000 acres. Open 7 a.m. to dusk. Spring, fall best times. Visitor center open Fri.–Mon. Primitive camping; no water. Food and lodging nearby.

19 Ruby Lake N.W.R.
Ruby Valley, NV
89833
(702) 779-2234

Meadows, freshwater marsh, and open water, nourished by runoff from Ruby Mountains and some 130 springs. Noted for dense nesting populations of canvasbacks and redheads; also nesters such as trumpeter swans, greater sandhill cranes, and white-faced ibises; other birds such as Lewis' woodpeckers, bushtits, and marsh wrens.

37,630 acres. Open dawn to dusk. Spring, summer, fall best times. 35 campsites.

20 Sheldon N.W.R.
P.O. Box 111
Rm. 308
U.S. Post Office
    Bldg.
Lakeview, OR 97630
(702) 941-0200

High semidesert typical of Great Basin; tablelands, rolling hills, narrow valleys, and canyons. Pronghorns, bighorn sheep, mule deer; sagebrush, greasewood, juniper, aspen.

575,000 acres. Spring, summer, fall best times. Information at subheadquarters in Virgin Valley. 18 campsites.

21 Stillwater
   W.M.A
Box 1236
1510 Rio Vista Rd.
Fallon, NV 89406
(702) 423-5128

Marsh and lake tucked within a mountain basin and fed by runoff from the Sierra Nevada. Once a haven for numerous waterfowl, Stillwater now has few; high demand for irrigation, combined with droughts, occasionally turns much of wetlands into dry salt flats.

24,000 acres. Spring, fall best times. Information at Nevada Dept. of Wildlife, 380 W. B St., Fallon. Primitive camping.

22 Toiyabe N.F.
1200 Franklin Way
Sparks, NV 89431
(702) 784-5331

Varied terrain of pine and aspen woods, rugged high country, desert, limestone cliffs, canyons and valleys, lakes and streams. Ghost towns. Includes Hoover Wilderness.

3,195,332 acres, part in CA. Wilderness area accessible only in July and Aug.; permits required. Information at ranger stations in Austin, Bridgeport, Carson City, Las Vegas, and Tonopah. 846 campsites, some year-round. Food and lodging nearby.

New Hampshire

Autumn's paintbox brings the rolling White Mountain National Forest to its fullest glory. On clear days, mountaintop Wapack National Wildlife Refuge offers a splendid panoramic view.

•Concord

---

1 **Appalachian N.S.T.**   *see* Maine

2 **Wapack N.W.R.**
Weir Hill Rd.
Sudbury, MA 01776
(617) 443-4661

Mountain site near Appalachian N.S.T. where migrating red-tailed hawks may be spotted; more common are nesting white-throated sparrows.

1,672 acres. Spring, summer, fall best times. Great Meadows Visitor Center. Food and lodging nearby.

3 **White Mountain N.F.**
Federal Building
719 Main St.
P.O. Box 638
Laconia, NH 03246
(603) 524-6450

Dense forest of birch and sugar maple covers rolling mountains in heart of New England. Magnificent autumn foliage. Lakes and streams; covered bridges. Great Gulf Wilderness.

728,623 acres, part in ME. Reservations accepted for Barnes Field camping area. Information at ranger stations in Compton, Conway, and Lincoln. Cabins; 938 campsites, many open mid-May–mid-Oct., some year round. Food and lodging nearby.

New Jersey

Among the nation's wildlife refuges, New Jersey's Brigantine proves a favorite with naturalists; Great Swamp, near New York City, is a wet, wooded haven for some 200 bird species.

1 **Appalachian N.S.T.**   *see* Maine

2 **Barnegat N.W.R.**
700 W. Bay Ave.
P.O. Box 544
Barnegat, NJ
08005
(609) 698-1387

Salt marsh, bay, creeks, and hardwood swamps. Gulls, wading birds, and shorebirds common in summer; waterfowl and birds of prey in winter.

10,200 acres. Open dawn to dusk. Spring, fall best times. Food and lodging nearby.

3 **Brigantine N.W.R.**
Great Creek Rd.
Box 72
Oceanville, NJ
08231
(609) 652-1665

Chiefly wetland along shore of southern New Jersey; huge flocks of ducks and geese in fall; skimmers, willets, herons, egrets, other waders and shorebirds in spring and summer.

20,197 acres. Open dawn to dusk. Spring, fall best times. Photo blinds available by permit. Food and lodging nearby.

4 **Delaware Water Gap N.R.A.**   *see* Pennsylvania

5 **Gateway N.R.A.**   *see* New York

6 **Great Swamp N.W.R.**
Pleasant Plains Rd.
R.D. 1, Box 152
Basking Ridge, NJ
07920
(201) 677-1222

Marshes, timbered swamps, and uplands attracting waterfowl such as wood ducks, green-winged and blue-winged teal, Canada geese. Some 200 species of birds thrive here, among them killdeer, kestrels, bitterns; also mammals such as white-tailed deer, minks, foxes.

6,783 acres. Open dawn to dusk. Spring, fall best times. Photo blinds available. Food and lodging nearby.

WHITE SANDS NATIONAL MONUMENT, NEW MEXICO

New Mexico

Ancient pueblo ruins, 17th-century mission churches, and ghost towns built on gold and silver await visitors to New Mexico's history-rich sites. With a third of its area under federal stewardship, the "Land of Enchantment" abounds in natural spectacles: the lofty underground chambers of Carlsbad Caverns; shimmering waves of gypsum at White Sands National Monument; flocks of sandhill cranes at the Bosque del Apache refuge.

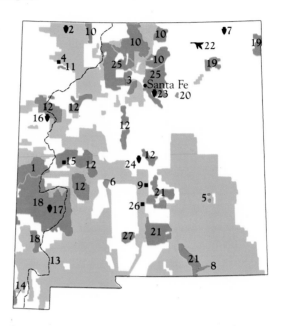

1 **Apache-Sitgreaves N.F.**

see Arizona

2 **Aztec Ruins N.M.**
P.O. Box U
Aztec, NM 87410
(505) 334-6174

Ruins of one of the largest pre-Columbian Indian villages built of masonry and timber. Misnamed by early settlers who attributed them to the Aztecs of Mexico.

27 acres. Entrance fee. Visitor center: interpretive exhibits. Food and lodging nearby.

3 **Bandelier N.M.**
Los Alamos, NM 87544
(505) 672-3861

Cliff houses of 12th-15th-century Pueblo Indians carved into steep-walled canyons. Named for a Swiss scientist, the first person to study the ruins.

32,737 acres. Trails not cleared of snow in winter. Entrance fee; reservations for group camping. Visitor center: exhibits; interpretive and audiovisual campfire programs and other activities in summer. 54 campsites; food services. Food and lodging nearby.

4 Bisti
Bureau of Land
Management
P.O. Box 6770
Albuquerque, NM
87107
(505) 766-2455

Badlands lying between Farmington and Crownpoint. Colorful mound and tower formations; petrified logs; fossilized dinosaur bones. Plants primarily cactuses and greasewood; animals include hawks, eagles, rabbits, lizards.

3,968 acres. Fall, spring best times. Information at BLM office in Farmington.

5 Bitter Lake N.W.R.
Box 7
Roswell, NM 88201
(505) 622-6755

2 tracts in Pecos River Valley. Salt Creek Wilderness. Bitter Lake and man-made ponds attract thousands of ducks, geese, and sandhill cranes during fall migration. Scenic red bluff; gypsum sinkholes.

23,350 acres. Open 1 hour before sunrise–1 hour after sunset. Spring, fall best times. Primitive camping. Food and lodging nearby.

6 Bosque del Apache N.W.R.
Box 1246
Socorro, NM 87801
(505) 835-1828

Woodlands and marsh where whooping cranes winter with their sandhill crane foster parents; ducks and snow geese in late fall and winter; abundant mule deer.

57,191 acres. Open half hour before sunrise to half hour after sunset. Fall, winter best times. Photo blinds may be reserved.

7 Capulin Mountain N.M.
Capulin, NM 88414
(505) 278-2201

Views of 4 states—New Mexico, Colorado, Oklahoma, and Texas—from summit of Capulin Mountain, an extinct volcano.

775 acres. Road closed occasionally by snow. Entrance fee; permits obtained at visitor center. Interpretive and audiovisual programs. Food and lodging nearby.

8 Carlsbad Caverns N.P.
3225 National Parks Hwy.
Carlsbad, NM 88220
(505) 785-2232

Among the world's largest and most spectacular limestone caverns. One of the underground chambers, Big Room, covers about 14 acres. Dramatic stalagmite-stalactite formations. Huge bat population; bats fly out of cave nightly in summer.

46,755 acres. Cave open 8 a.m.–4:30 p.m. in winter; 8–5:30 in spring; 7:30–7:30 in summer. Entrance fee. Visitor center: cave tours; exhibits. Food services. No pets or very young children allowed in caverns; kennel and nursery available. Food and lodging nearby.

9 Carrizozo Malpais

Bureau of Land Management
P.O. Box 1397
Roswell, NM 88201
(505) 622-7670

Lava flow almost 1,500 years old—among the most recent in continental U. S.; originated at Little Black Peak. Extremely rugged surface, with diverse vegetation; inhabited by mule deer, Barbary sheep, dark-colored rodents and reptiles. 3 miles west of Carrizozo.

25,000 acres. Spring, fall best times. Information at Valley of Fires State Park. Food and lodging nearby.

10 Carson N.F.

Forest Service Bldg.
P.O. Box 558
Taos, NM 87571
(505) 758-2238

Timbered Sangre de Cristo Mountains flanking upper Rio Grande Valley. Alpine lakes; trout streams; valleys. Spanish-speaking villages. Includes 4 wilderness areas.

1,491,515 acres. Permits required for Pecos Wilderness. Information at ranger stations in Blanco, Canjilon, El Rito, Penasco, Questa, Taos, and Tres Piedras. 387 campsites, most open Apr./May–Sept./Oct., some year round; food services. No drinking water in some camping areas. Food and lodging nearby.

11 Chaco Culture N.H.P.

Star Route 4
Box 6500
Bloomfield, NM 87413
(505) 786-5384

13 major ruins and hundreds of smaller ones represent the culmination of pre-Columbian Pueblo civilization.

33,989 acres. Open sunrise to sunset. Permits required for backcountry use; no overnight backpacking. Visitor center: interpretive programs, exhibits; campfire talks, walking tours, guided tours. 46 campsites.

12 Cibola N.F.

10308 Candelaria Rd., N.E.
Albuquerque, NM 87112
(505) 766-2185

High forested mountain ranges surrounded by desert grasslands. Spruce, fir, juniper, and pine. Fishing lakes. Ghost towns. Pueblo Indian villages nearby, including the "Sky City" of Acoma, continuously inhabited since the 13th century; also prehistoric ruins.

1,635,500 acres. Information at ranger stations in Clayton, Grants, Magdalena, Mountainair, and Tijeras, NM; Cheyenne, OK; Texline, TX. 273 campsites, most open Apr.–Oct.; food services; aerial tram to Sandia Peak. Most pueblos in good condition are privately owned and occupied and not open to public. Food and lodging nearby.

13 Continental Divide N.S.T.

see Montana

14 Coronado N.F.

see Arizona

15 Datil Well Campground
Bureau of Land Management
P.O. Box 1219
Socorro, NM 87801
(505) 835-0412

Well on Magdalena Livestock Driveway was water source for pioneers heading west in 1880s; last cattle drive held in 1960s. Scenic vistas; piñon-juniper forests.

640 acres. Apr.–Oct. best time. 22 campsites. Food and lodging nearby.

16 El Morro N.M.
Ramah, NM 87321
(505) 783-5132

Sandstone cliff above a rocky pool bears inscriptions of desert travelers from Spanish Juan de Oñate in 1605 to 19th-century pioneers; carvings by pre-Columbian Indians.

1,279 acres. Open 8 a.m.–5 p.m.; to 8 p.m. in summer. Mesa Top Trail closed during heavy snow; when campground closed by snow, campers can park at HQ. Entrance fee. Walking tours, campfire programs in summer. 9 campsites. Food nearby.

17 Gila Cliff Dwellings N.M.
Route 11, Box 100
Silver City, NM 88061
(505) 534-9344

Well-preserved ruins of rooms built within natural cavities in cliff wall, 180 feet above canyon floor; inhabited A.D. 100–1300.

533 acres. Open 8 a.m.–6 p.m. Memorial Day–Labor Day; 9 a.m.–4 p.m. rest of year. Visitor center. Forest Service campgrounds, food, and lodging nearby.

18 Gila N.F.
2610 N. Silver St.
Silver City, NM 88061
(505) 388-1986

Mountainous area surrounded by high desert. Juniper, pine, spruce, aspen, cactuses, and grasses. Canyons, mesas, lakes, and streams. 3 wilderness areas.

2,705,752 acres. Permits required for backcountry use and for boating on Lower San Francisco River. Information at ranger stations in Glenwood, Luna, Magdalena, Mimbres, Quemado, Reserve, Silver City, and Truth or Consequences. 181 campsites, most open Apr. to Nov., some year round. Food and lodging nearby.

19 Kiowa N.G.
16 N. 2nd St.
Clayton, NM 88415
(505) 374-9652

Flat to rolling grassy plains; part of the Canadian River Canyon. Mills Canyon forms a habitat for mule deer, bears, Barbary sheep, Siberian ibexes, ducks, and geese.

136,505 acres. Spring, summer best times. Access road to Mills Canyon is primitive; 4-wheel-drive vehicle necessary. 8 campsites. Food and lodging nearby.

20 **Las Vegas N.W.R.**
Route 1, Box 399
Las Vegas, NM
87701
(505) 425-3581

Sweeping grasslands and plunging canyons, noted for large gatherings of birds of prey; prairie falcons year-round; endangered peregrine falcons migrate through; Swainson's and red-tailed hawks in spring and fall.

8,754 acres. Open dawn to dusk. Fall, winter best times. Permits required for nature trail. Food and lodging nearby.

21 **Lincoln N.F.**
Federal Building
11th and New York
Sts.
Alamogordo, NM
88310
(505) 437-6030

Mountains covered with stands of pine and fir in dry country. Many undeveloped caves. Includes White Mountain and Capitan Mountain Wilderness Areas, with varied life zones. Temperature drops sharply at night above 7,000 feet.

1,103,441 acres. Reservations required for group campgrounds. Information at ranger stations in Carlsbad, Cloudcroft, Mayhill, and Ruidoso. 368 campsites, most open May–Sept. No drinking water in some camping areas. Food and lodging nearby.

22 **Maxwell N.W.R.**
Box 276
Maxwell, NM 87728
(505) 375-2331

Grasslands, lakes, and farm tracts nearly encircled by mountains. Birds of prey abound, including prairie falcons, bald and golden eagles, and ferruginous hawks; numerous songbirds, geese, and ducks.

3,584 acres. Spring, fall, winter best times. Campsites. Food and lodging nearby.

23 **Pecos N.M.**
P.O. Drawer 11
Pecos, NM 87552
(505) 757-6414

Historic landmark on Santa Fe Trail. Ruins of 17th-century mission church; ancient Indian pueblo; restored kivas.

365 acres. Spring, early summer best times. Visitor center: walking tours; Indian craft demonstrations on summer weekends; living history demonstrations only in summer. Food and lodging nearby.

24 **Salinas N.M.**
P.O. Box 496
Mountainair, NM
87036
(505) 847-2585

Regional complex of large prehistoric and historic Pueblo Indian villages and five 17th-century mission ruins at Abo, Quarai, and Gran Quivira.

1,080 acres. Open 8 a.m.–5 p.m.; Gran Quivira entrance gate closed at sunset. Summer, fall best times. Information at 3 ruin sites and at HQ in historic Shaffer Hotel in Mountainair; exhibits, tours. Food and lodging nearby.

25 Santa Fe N.F.
1220 St. Francis Dr.
P.O. Box 1689
Santa Fe, NM 87501
(505) 988-6940

Stands of aspen, pine, fir, and spruce covering Sangre de Cristo and Jemez Mountains; geologic formations; fishing streams and high-country lakes; 4 wilderness areas. Prehistoric pueblo ruins.

·1,589,000 acres. Permits required for 2 wilderness areas; reservations required for group camping areas. Information at ranger stations in Coyote, Cuba, Espanola, Jemez Springs, Las Vegas, Pecos, and Santa Fe. 512 campsites, open May to Oct. Food and lodging nearby.

26 Three Rivers Petroglyph Site
Bureau of Land Management
P.O. Box 1420
1705 N. Valley Dr.
Las Cruces, NM 88001
(505) 523-5571

More than 5,000 rock carvings of masks, wildlife, and geometric designs made by Jornada Mogollon people, hunters and farmers from A.D. 900 to 1400. One of the largest petroglyph sites in the Southwest, 3 miles northeast of Three Rivers.

960 acres. 6 campsites.

27 White Sands N.M.
P.O. Box 458
Alamogordo, NM 88310
(505) 437-1058

Gleaming white landscape of wavelike gypsum sand dunes; habitat of white lizard and mouse species that have permanently changed color and match their surroundings.

144,420 acres. Entrance fee; registration required for camping. Visitor center: museum; guided walks, illustrated evening programs, star programs in summer. Dunes Drive open 8 a.m.–10 p.m. (to midnight during full moon), May 27–Sept. 3; 8:30 a.m.–half hour after sunset, rest of year. Primitive camping; food services. Food and lodging nearby.

New York

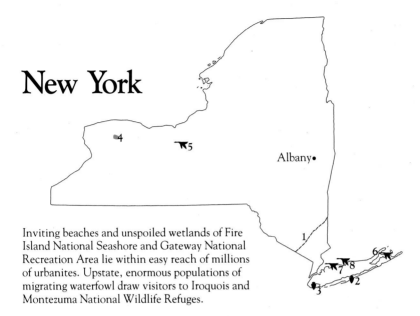

Albany•

Inviting beaches and unspoiled wetlands of Fire Island National Seashore and Gateway National Recreation Area lie within easy reach of millions of urbanites. Upstate, enormous populations of migrating waterfowl draw visitors to Iroquois and Montezuma National Wildlife Refuges.

1 **Appalachian N.S.T.** *see* Maine

2 **Fire Island N.S.**
120 Laurel St.
Patchogue, NY 11772
(516) 289-4810

Roadless barrier island, 32 miles long, off south shore of Long Island. Thickets, salt marshes, grassy wetlands. Wildlife watching.

19,579 acres. Access by ferry or private boat. Open 8 a.m.–6 p.m. Marinas and visitor centers closed in winter. Permits for off-road vehicle travel; reservations required for Watch Hill campsite. Visitor centers: guided nature walks and talks in summer; interpretive exhibits. Rooms; 29 campsites; food services. Food and lodging nearby.

3 **Gateway N.R.A.**
Floyd Bennett Field
Bldg. 69
Brooklyn, NY 11234
(212) 338-3338

Urban park comprising Jamaica Bay unit in Brooklyn, Jamaica Bay Wildlife Refuge and Breezy Point unit in Queens, Staten Island unit, and Sandy Hook unit in northeastern New Jersey.

26,645 acres, part in NJ. Full services provided from Memorial Day through Sept. 30, 9 a.m.–8:30 p.m. Permits for sports facilities at Miller Field; reservations for organized youth group camping. Information at HQ; interpretive programs; cultural, historical, and recreational special events. Camping for school groups only; food services in summer. Food and lodging nearby.

4 **Iroquois N.W.R.**
P.O. Box 517
Alabama, NY 14003
(716) 958-5445

Swamp, timberland, grassland, and cropland with ponds and marshes, where immense flocks of migrating Canada geese gather; large numbers of wood ducks; tundra swans; white-tailed deer, foxes, muskrats, beavers, wild turkeys.

10,818 acres. Open dawn to dusk. Spring, fall best times. Photo blinds may be reserved. Food and lodging nearby.

5 **Montezuma N.W.R.**
3395 Route 5/20 E.
Seneca Falls, NY 13148
(315) 568-5987

Mainly swamp and wetland, with small stands of timber scattered along uplands. Bald eagles sighted occasionally in spring and fall; huge flocks of migrating Canada and snow geese and large numbers of ducks in spring; white-tailed deer.

6,432 acres. Open daylight hours. Spring, fall best times. Permits required for closed area. Visitor center. Food and lodging nearby.

6 **Morton N.W.R.**
R.D. 359, Noyac Rd.
Sag Harbor, NY 11963
(516) 725-2270

Northern two-thirds is peninsula known as Jessups Neck, fringed by sandy, gravelly, and rocky beaches; wooded bluffs overlook brackish pond. Remainder is woodland, brush, and open fields. More than 200 species of waterfowl, birds of prey, shorebirds, and songbirds recorded here.

187 acres. Open 9 a.m.–5 p.m. Spring, fall best times. Food and lodging nearby.

7 **Oyster Bay N.W.R.**
Box 21
Shirley, NY 11967
(516) 286-0485

Refuge is mainly the bay bottom and lands up to mean high water. Mill Neck Creek and Frost Creek salt marsh areas provide resting sites for wintering waterfowl.

3,117 acres. Winter best time. Food and lodging nearby.

8 **Target Rock N.W.R.**
P.O. Box 21
Shirley, NY 11967
(516) 286-0485

Walking trails pass through hardwood forests and old formal gardens and by a small pond and the shore of Huntington Bay. Variety of birds and mammals; spring warbler migration coincides with bloom in old gardens.

80 acres. Open 9 a.m.–5 p.m. Spring, fall best times. Permission required to visit. Food and lodging nearby.

North Carolina

The oldest national seashore, Cape Hatteras, and its more southerly counterpart, Cape Lookout, together comprise the East Coast's longest stretch of protected shoreline. These barrier islands and the state's national wildlife refuges are important wintering grounds for migratory waterfowl. Near the western border, the Blue Ridge Parkway traverses mountainous Pisgah National Forest.

1 **Appalachian N.S.T.** *see* Maine

2 **Cape Hatteras N.S.**
Route 1, Box 675
Manteo, NC 27954
(919) 473-2111

America's first national seashore, on North Carolina's Outer Banks. Cape Hatteras Lighthouse overlooks the "graveyard of the Atlantic," area of many shipwrecks over the centuries. Wildlife refuge.

30,319 acres. Reservations available for several campgrounds in summer. Whalebone Junction Information Center; several visitor centers; interpretive exhibits; guided walks and evening talks in summer. 715 campsites; all campgrounds closed Nov.–Mar.; Frisco and Salvo campgrounds closed Labor Day–Memorial Day. Food and lodging nearby.

3 **Cape Lookout N.S.**
P.O. Box 690
Beaufort, NC 28516
(919) 728-2121

Chain of barrier islands, composed of beaches, island dunes, and marshes, extending 58 miles along lower Outer Banks. Shell collecting; bird watching. Historic sites include Portsmouth Village, Cape Lookout Lighthouse.

28,400 acres. Ferry fee. Information at seashore HQ in Beaufort; interpretive programs in summer. Rustic cabins; primitive camping. Bring insect repellent and water. Food nearby.

4 Cedar Island N.W.R.
Route 1, Box N-2
Swanquarter, NC
27885
(919) 926-4021

Island bounded by Core and Pamlico Sounds; mainly salt marsh. Nesting site for black ducks; also attracts various songbirds and mammals.

12,526 acres. Open dawn to dusk. Information at Mattamuskeet N.W.R. Food nearby.

5 Croatan N.F.
435 Thurman Rd.
New Bern, NC
28560
(919) 638-5628

Working loblolly and longleaf pine forest. Peat swamps with unusual flora such as pitcher plants and Venus's-flytraps. Bays, creeks, and marshes attract migratory waterfowl.

157,063 acres. Information at ranger station in New Bern. 72 campsites, open Mar.–Oct. Food and lodging nearby.

6 Great Dismal Swamp N.W.R.

see Virginia

7 Great Smoky Mountains N.P.

see Tennessee

8 Mackay Island N.W.R.
P.O. Box 31
Knotts Island, NC
27950
(919) 429-3100

Brackish marsh and woodland swamp attract Canada and snow geese, black ducks, other migrating waterfowl; also many small songbirds.

7,056 acres, part in VA. Open Mar. 15–Oct. 15, dawn to dusk. Food and lodging nearby.

9 Mattamuskeet N.W.R.
Route 1, Box N-2
Swanquarter, NC
27885
(919) 926-4021

Lake Mattamuskeet, 18 miles long and 6 miles wide, fringed by marsh and timberland; huge population of tundra swans winters here; also ducks and Canada geese.

50,177 acres. Open dawn to dusk. Winter best time. Food and lodging nearby.

10 Nantahala N.F.
B Level Plateau
Bldg.
50 S. French Broad
Ave.
P.O. Box 2750
Asheville, NC 28802
(704) 253-2352

Mountains; deep, narrow valleys and gulleys; canyons; waterfalls; hardwood forests. Includes Joyce Kilmer-Slickrock Wilderness, with azaleas, rhododendrons, and more than 100 varieties of trees.

515,492 acres. Information at ranger stations in Franklin, Highlands, Murphy, and Robbinsville. 365 campsites; food services. Food and lodging nearby.

11 Pea Island N.W.R.
Box 150
Rodanthe, NC
27968
(919) 987-2394

Long, narrow island on Outer Banks. Beaches, dunes, ponds, and mud flats attract varied wildlife, including greater snow geese, 26 duck species, and rare brown pelicans; water birds such as skimmers, terns, and gulls; also muskrats and otters.

5,915 acres. Open dawn to dusk. Food and lodging nearby.

12 Pee Dee N.W.R.
Box 780
Wadesboro, NC
28170
(704) 694-4424

Habitat for ducks and geese in winter and sanctuary for red-cockaded woodpeckers; foxes, beavers, and bobcats often sighted.

8,443 acres. Refuge open year round, dawn to dusk; sanctuary closed Sept.–Apr. Information at refuge office, U.S. 52, Wadesboro. 2 photo blinds on waterfowl impoundments. Food and lodging nearby.

13 Pisgah N.F.
B Level Plateau
Bldg.
50 S. French Broad
Ave.
P.O. Box 2750
Asheville, NC 28802
(704) 253-2352

Mountain slopes densely timbered with mixed hardwoods; steep gorges; delicate waterfalls; azaleas and purple rhododendron. Exceptional spring and fall displays. 2 wilderness areas.

495,712 acres. Reservations required for Linville Gorge Wilderness. Visitor center on U.S. 279. 482 campsites, most open Apr./May to late fall. Food and lodging nearby.

14 Pungo N.W.R.
Box 267
Plymouth, NC 27962
(919) 793-2143

Pungo Lake and surrounding marsh and timbered swamp. Home to Canada and snow geese, tundra swans, and some dozen duck species; various small birds common seasonally.

12,300 acres. Open daylight hours. Mar.–Nov. best time. Food and lodging nearby.

15 Swanquarter N.W.R.
Route 1, Box N-2
Swanquarter, NC
27885
(919) 926-4021

Marsh and timbered swamp fronting Pamlico Sound. Numerous waterfowl, including redhead, scaup, and canvasback ducks; occasional sightings of bears and alligators.

15,643 acres. Open dawn to dusk. Apr.–June best time. Information at Mattamuskeet N.W.R. Food and lodging nearby.

16 Uwharrie N.F.
N.C. Hwy. 27
Troy, NC 27371
(919) 576-6391

Small, working mixed pine and hardwood forest on rolling mountain slopes in rich piedmont. Fishing lake and river.

46,767 acres. 36 campsites, open May–Oct. No drinking water in West Morris Mountain Camp area. Food and lodging nearby.

North Dakota

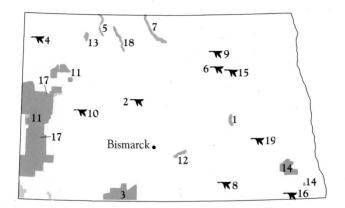

An extraordinary profusion of bird species finds prime nesting habitat amid the glacier-scoured wetlands of North Dakota's national wildlife refuges. "Barren, fantastic and grimly picturesque deserts," President Theodore Roosevelt called the multi-hued badlands in the national park that bears his name.

1 Arrowwood N.W.R.
Rural Route 1
Pingree, ND 58476
(701) 285-3341

Tableland laced with gullies and nourished by 4 lakes; visited by great numbers of migrating waterfowl in spring and fall; abundant white-tailed deer, badgers, and foxes; sharp-tailed grouse perform courting dances in spring.

15,934 acres. Open dawn to dusk; closed during Oct. for waterfowl. Spring, fall best times.

2 Audubon N.W.R.
Rural Route 1
Coleharbor, ND 58531
(701) 442-5474

Fertile prairie with hills and glacier-carved ponds; Lake Audubon sprinkled with some 150 islands. Nesting water birds, including black-crowned night herons, avocets, and Canada geese; white-tailed deer common.

14,735 acres. Open dawn to dusk. Spring, fall best times. Photo blinds available. Food and lodging nearby.

3 Cedar River N.G.
Grand River Ranger District
P.O. Box 390
Lemmon, SD 57638
(605) 374-3592

Rolling shortgrass and midgrass prairie. Wildlife includes deer, pronghorns, waterfowl, sharp-tailed grouse.

6,237 acres. June, Sept.–Oct. best times. Interior not accessible by passenger car.

THEODORE ROOSEVELT NATIONAL PARK, NORTH DAKOTA

4 **Crosby W.M.D.**
Box 148
Crosby, ND 58730
(701) 965-6488

Includes 92 waterfowl production areas and Lake Zahl N.W.R. Ducks, Canada geese, marsh birds, shorebirds, and birds of prey breed here; whooping cranes and sandhill cranes visit in spring and fall; sharp-tailed grouse gather on "dancing grounds" in spring.

85,819 acres. Spring, fall best times. Permission from landowners required for using easement lands. Food and lodging nearby.

5 **Des Lacs N.W.R.**
Box 578
Kenmare, ND 58746
(701) 385-4046

Marshes and lakes attracting shorebirds and waterfowl; grasslands and woods filled with birds such as Sprague's pipits, lark buntings, and veeries; also white-tailed deer, coyotes, red foxes, beavers, and muskrats.

18,881 acres. Open dawn to dusk; sometimes closed for sanctuary during hunting season. Spring, summer, fall best times. Reservations required for photo blinds. Food and lodging nearby.

6 **Devils Lake W.M.D.**
218 S.W. 4th St.
Box 908
Devils Lake, ND 58301
(701) 662-8611

Encompasses wetland areas in 8 counties; abounds in waterfowl, deer, moose, and elk.

197,555 acres. Open dawn to dusk. Spring, fall best times. Primitive camping. Food and lodging nearby.

7 **J. Clark Salyer N.W.R.**
Upham, ND 58789
(701) 768-2548

Extensive marshlands and grasslands with thickets and timberland, home to more than 250 bird species. Shorebirds include yellowlegs and northern phalaropes; white pelicans summer here; large numbers of waterfowl; famous for viewing Le Conte's sparrows.

58,693 acres. Open 5 a.m.–10 p.m. Spring, fall best times. Photo blind available on sharp-tailed grouse dancing ground.

8 **Kulm W.M.D.**
Box E
Kulm, ND 58456
(701) 647-2866

Oversees waterfowl production areas and a few small refuges located in 4 counties of North Dakota; major nesting area for many duck species.

42,352 acres. Open dawn to dusk. Spring, fall best times. Food and lodging nearby.

9 **Lake Alice N.W.R.**
Box 908
Devil's Lake, ND 58301
(701) 662-8611

3,400 shallow lakes surrounded by flat grassland. Nesting waterfowl; white-tailed deer.

10,772 acres. Open dawn to dusk. Spring, fall best times. Primitive camping. Food and lodging nearby.

10 Lake Ilo N.W.R.
c/o Des Lacs
N.W.R.
P.O. Box 578
Kenmare, ND
58746
(701) 385-4046

1,100-acre lake surrounded by grasslands used for nesting. Waterfowl include Canada geese and many duck species.

3,739 acres. Open dawn to dusk. Spring, fall best times. Information at Des Lacs N.W.R. Food and lodging nearby.

11 Little Missouri N.G.
Route 3, Box 131-B
Dickenson, ND
58601
(701) 225-5152

Shortgrass prairie and badlands. Wildlife includes deer, pronghorns, grouse, bighorn sheep. Burning Coal Vein has been alight since white men first came to the area.

1,027,852 acres. Summer, fall best times. Some roads very muddy at times. Information at Medora Ranger Station. 40 campsites. Food and lodging nearby.

12 Long Lake N.W.R.
Rural Route 1
Moffit, ND 58560
(701) 387-4397

Concentrations of ducks and geese visit this lake set in rolling prairie and cultivated uplands. Sandhill cranes migrate through in sizable flocks during Sept. and Oct.

22,300 acres. Apr.–May, Sept.–Oct. best times. Information at Arrowwood N.W.R. Food and lodging nearby.

13 Lostwood N.W.R.
Rural Route 2
Box 98
Kenmare, ND 58746
(701) 848-2722

Prairie dotted with glacial wetlands and small groves of aspen. Shorebirds, waterfowl, and birds of prey; small birds such as Sprague's pipits, Le Conte's and Baird's sparrows.

26,747 acres. Open dawn to dusk. May–June best times.

14 Sheyenne N.G.
P.O. Box 943
Lisbon, ND 58054
(701) 683-4342

Undulating sandhills; tallgrass to midgrass prairie. Wildlife includes greater prairie-chickens, pheasants, waterfowl, and white-tailed deer.

70,180 acres. Spring, summer best times. Food and lodging nearby.

15 Sullys Hill National Game Preserve
Fort Totten, ND
58335
(701) 662-8611

Glacial moraine hills, covered with brush and woodland, set aside to protect bison and other large game animals; now bison, white-tailed deer, and elk thrive here.

1,674 acres. Open May–Nov., 8 a.m. to dusk, and in other months as road conditions allow. Spring, fall best times. Food and lodging nearby.

16 Tewaukon N.W.R.
Rural Route 1
Cayuga, ND 58013
(701) 724-3598

Prairie, marsh, and wetland spotted with glacial ponds; numerous water birds visit, among them several duck and heron species; white-tailed deer year round.

8,444 acres. Open dawn to dusk. Spring, fall best times.

17 Theodore Roosevelt N.P.
P.O. Box 7
Medora, ND 58645
(701) 623-4466

Scenic badlands along Little Missouri River contain cabin from Theodore Roosevelt's Maltese Cross Ranch and site of his Elkhorn Ranch. Bison and bird watching.

70,416 acres. Some parts closed in winter. May–Oct. best time. Entrance fee; permits available for backcountry; reservations required for group camping. Visitor center: interpretive exhibits, guided walks, campfire programs. 150 campsites. Food and lodging nearby.

18 Upper Souris N.W.R.
Rural Route 1
Foxholm, ND 58738
(701) 468-5634

Blend of prairie, marsh, lakes, and woods fronting the Souris River. Water birds flock here, including Canada geese, wood ducks, and black-crowned night herons; abundant white-tailed deer and minks.

32,000 acres. Open 5 a.m.–10 p.m. Spring, fall best times. Food nearby.

19 Valley City W.M.D.
Rural Route 1
Valley City, ND 58072
(701) 845-3466

72 units in prairie pothole region. Eastern third is flat and extensively farmed; remainder is rolling drift prairie. Wetlands attract geese, tundra swans, other waterfowl in spring and fall; mallards, gadwalls, blue-winged teal nest here; mammals include deer, foxes, beavers, squirrels.

16,198 acres. Spring, fall best times. Information at Arrowwood N.W.R. Food and lodging nearby.

Ohio

Between bustling Cleveland and Akron, Cuyahoga Valley National Recreation Area preserves a pastoral, history-filled environment. Prehistoric burial sites at Mound City Group yield insights into the rich culture of the Hopewell Indians.

1 Cuyahoga Valley N.R.A.
15610 Vaughn Rd.
Brecksville, OH 44141
(216) 650-4636

Scenic stretch of rural Cuyahoga Valley. Ohio and Erie Canal System. Golf, skating, sledding.

32,000 acres. Some areas closed at dusk; Blossom Music Center and Porthouse Theater open in summer only; Hale Farm and Village open May–Oct., Dec. Canal Visitor Center; Happy Days Visitor Center; interpretive exhibits. Food and lodging nearby.

2 Mound City Group N.M.
16062 State Route 104
Chillicothe, OH 45601
(614) 744-1125

Largest known concentration of Hopewell Indian burial mounds, heaped up about 2,000 years ago and containing copper breastplates, ceremonial pipes, fine jewelry, and pottery shards.

120 acres. Open dawn to dusk. Visitor center: interpretive exhibits. Food and lodging nearby.

3 Ottawa N.W.R.
14000 W. State Route 2
Oak Harbor, OH 43449
(419) 898-0014

Stands of timber amid marshland that attracts pheasants and waterfowl; tundra swans, ducks, and geese migrate in spring and fall; great egrets and great blue and night herons also abundant in those seasons.

5,794 acres. Open dawn to dusk. Spring, summer, fall best times. Photo blinds available. Food and lodging nearby.

4 Wayne N.F.
3527 10th St.
Bedford, IN 47421
(812) 275-5987

Timbered, rolling hills; wildlife; spring and fall color. Includes Civil War iron-producing area.

176,000 acres. Spring, fall best times. Visitor center at Lake Vesuvius. 86 campsites, some open mid-May–mid-Sept., some year round. Food and lodging nearby.

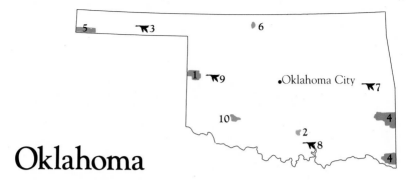

Oklahoma

A favored destination of Oklahomans and Texans, Chickasaw National Recreation Area embraces a large reservoir and a network of trails near the scenic Arbuckle Mountains. Among the state's national wildlife refuges, Wichita Mountains enjoys widespread fame for its prairie dog town and large herds of bison, elk, and Texas longhorn cattle.

1 Black Kettle N.G.
P.O. Box 266
Cheyenne, OK
73628
(405) 497-2143

Rolling hills with midgrass to tallgrass prairie and some timber. Wildlife includes deer, wild turkeys, and bobwhite quail. Marvin, Skipout, Spring Creek, and Dead Indian Lakes form major recreation area.

31,000 acres, part in TX. Sept.–Oct. best time. Fee for use of Lake Marvin. 48 campsites. Food and lodging nearby.

2 Chickasaw N.R.A.
P.O. Box 201
Sulphur, OK 73086
(405) 622-3161

Man-made Lake of the Arbuckles, accessible from Oklahoma City and Dallas-Fort Worth area; numerous mineral and freshwater springs. Water sports.

9,500 acres. Tornadoes and thunderstorms Apr.–June. Camping permits required; reservations for group camping. Nature center: interpretive exhibits, guided nature walks, campfire programs, nature film. 461 campsites. Food and lodging nearby.

3 Optima N.W.R.
Rural Route 1
Box 68
Butler, OK 73625
(405) 473-2205

Grassland, sand sage, and woods; numerous mammals, among them pronghorns, coyotes, and mule and white-tailed deer; migrating waterfowl; golden and bald eagles.

4,333 acres. Open daylight hours. Spring, fall best times. Information at Corps of Engineers office near Optima Dam and at Washita N.W.R. Food and lodging nearby.

| 4 | **Ouachita N.F.** | *see* Arkansas |

| 5 | **Rita Blanca N.G.** | *see* Texas |

6 Salt Plains N.W.R.
Route 1, Box 76
Jet, OK 73749
(405) 626-4794

Salt flat, delta land, thick brush and woods, and open water. Whooping cranes in fall; scissor-tailed flycatchers in warmer months; abundant white-tailed deer and beavers.

31,997 acres. Open dawn to dusk. Fall best time. 20 campsites. Food and lodging nearby.

7 Sequoyah N.W.R.
Route 1, Box 18A
Vian, OK 74962
(918) 773-5251

Fertile bottomland, a sprinkling of islands, and rugged upland at junction of Arkansas and Canadian Rivers. Waterfowl in spring, fall, and winter; a number of eagles through fall and winter.

20,800 acres. Open 4 a.m.–10 p.m. Spring, fall, winter best times. Food and lodging nearby.

8 Tishomingo N.W.R.
Route 1, Box 152
Tishomingo, OK 73460
(405) 371-2402

Grassland, woodland, and farmland, with mud flats attracting white pelicans, geese, ducks, and many wading birds and shorebirds; white-tailed deer abundant; also bobcats, beavers, and raccoons.

16,464 acres. Open daylight hours. Fall, winter best times. Campsites. Food and lodging nearby.

9 Washita N.W.R.
Route 1, Box 68
Butler, OK 73625
(405) 473-2205

Grassland, cultivated fields, wood-fringed creeks, and open water, where huge numbers of waterfowl gather in winter; bald and golden eagles in winter; sandhill cranes and white pelicans in spring and fall.

8,200 acres. Open dawn to dusk. Late fall best time. 2 observation platforms; portable photo blinds allowed. Food nearby.

10 Wichita Mountains N.W.R.
Route 1, Box 448
Indiahoma, OK 73552
(405) 429-3222

Grassland with streams, lakes, and canyons; also mountains and forest. Set aside as sanctuary for bison, now also shelters elk and Texas longhorn cattle.

59,020 acres. Spring, fall best times. Campground; backcountry camping by permit; youth camping. Seasonally scheduled tours and hikes. Food and lodging nearby.

CRATER LAKE NATIONAL PARK, OREGON

Oregon

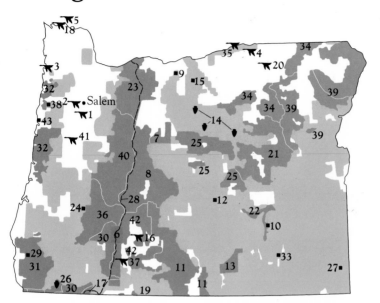

Covering more than half the state, Oregon's federal lands come together in a stunning quilt of snow-clad peaks, rolling sand dunes, dense forests, desert scrublands—and more. At Crater Lake National Park, the deepest body of water in the United States fills the caldera of a dormant volcano. Five geologic epochs are represented at John Day Fossil Beds; present-day fauna and flora in Oregon range from pronghorns and Columbian white-tailed deer to rare botanical specimens. Skiing, rock collecting, and white-water rafting are especially popular, as is fishing for abundant salmon and steelhead trout.

1 Ankeny N.W.R.
Route 2, Box 208
Corvallis, OR 97333
(503) 757-7236

Winter sanctuary for dusky Canada geese; marsh hawks, kestrels, and red-tailed hawks year round; migrators such as Swainson's and varied thrushes and tundra swans.

2,796 acres. Open daylight hours; goose habitat closed Nov. 1–Apr. 15. Spring, fall, winter best times. Information kiosk. Food and lodging nearby.

2 Baskett Slough N.W.R.
Route 2, Box 208
Corvallis, OR 97333
(503) 757-7236

Winter sanctuary for dusky Canada geese; marsh hawks, kestrels, and red-tailed hawks year round; migrators such as Swainson's and varied thrushes and tundra swans.

2,492 acres. Open daylight hours; goose habitat closed Oct. 1–May 1. Spring, fall, winter best times. Information kiosk. Food and lodging nearby.

3 Cape Meares N.W.R.
Route 2, Box 208
Corvallis, OR 97333
(503) 757-7236

Rugged shoreside terrain where thousands of seabirds nest in spring and fall; visitors such as tufted puffins, cormorants, and common murres; harbor seals and sea lions.

138 acres. Open daylight hours. Spring, summer, winter best times. Food and lodging nearby.

4 Cold Springs N.W.R.
P.O. Box 239
Umatilla, OR 97882
(503) 922-3232

Borders a reservoir and attracts great numbers of migrating ducks and other waterfowl; pelicans and swans winter here; deer commonly spotted.

3,117 acres. Spring, fall, winter best times. Food and lodging nearby.

5 Columbian White-tailed Deer N.W.R.
P.O. Box 566
Cathlamet, WA 98612
(206) 795-3915

Grasslands separated by woodlots of red alder, sitka spruce, and willow; set aside to protect Columbian white-tailed deer; also habitat for elk, coyotes, and migrating waterfowl.

4,800 acres, part in WA. Open dawn to dusk. Spring, fall, winter best times. Food and lodging nearby.

6 Crater Lake N.P.
P.O. Box 7
Crater Lake, OR 97604
(503) 594-2211

Deepest lake in U. S.—1,932 feet—in the heart of a collapsed volcano; encircles Wizard Island, a volcano within a volcano. Castle Crest Wildflower Garden near park headquarters.

183,180 acres. Open 24 hours a day in summer. North entrance road and Rim Drive closed mid-Oct.–early July depending on snowfall, which averages 50 ft. a year. Entrance fee. Information at park HQ and at visitor center; interpretive walks, talks. Rooms in summer; 212 campsites; food services; tour boat in summer.

7 Crooked River N.G.
2321 E. 3rd St.
Prineville, OR 97754
(503) 447-4120

Gently rolling terrain with juniper and sagebrush. Wildlife includes mule deer, pronghorns, falcons, golden and bald eagles. Prehistoric Indian sites. Rafting, other water sports in Deschutes River and Canyon.

105,224 acres. Summer best time. Muddy roads in winter and spring. 24 campsites. Food and lodging nearby.

8 Deschutes N.F.
211 N.E. Revere
Ave.
Bend, OR 97701
(503) 382-6922

Pine woodlands interspersed with meadows on eastern slopes of the Cascades. Lava beds, crater, caves, buttes, 301 lakes. Parts of 4 wilderness areas and Pacific Crest N.S.T.

1,602,609 acres. Reservations required for Little Fawn and Scout Lake camping areas and Chief Paulina, Quinn Meadow, and Sheep Springs horse camps. Information at ranger stations in Bend, Crescent, and Sisters. 100 campsites, most open May/June–Oct.; food services. Food and lodging nearby.

9 Deschutes River
Bureau of Land Management
P.O. Box 550
Prineville, OR 97754
(503) 447-4115

White-water river winding 80 miles through undulating terrain. Small game, deer, rodents, and waterfowl live amid sagebrush and grasses or along riverbanks.

10,000 acres. Spring, summer, fall best times. Boating fee. 37 campsites; primitive camping; food services. Food and lodging nearby.

10 Diamond Craters Natural Area
Bureau of Land Management
74 S. Alvord St.
Burns, OR 97720
(503) 573-5241

40-mile self-guided auto tour route explores diverse volcanic formations 55 miles southeast of Burns.

16,656 acres. Roads may be closed by snow in winter. Vehicle use limited to existing roads. Write for auto tour brochure. Food and lodging nearby.

11 Fremont N.F.
34 N. D St.
Lakeview, OR 97630
(503) 947-2151

Remote region on eastern slopes of the Cascades. Stands of pine broken by meadows and geologic formations; lakes, rivers; canyons, buttes. Gearhart Mountain Wilderness.

1,197,839 acres. Late Aug.–Sept. best time. Information at ranger stations in Bly, Lakeview, Paisley, and Silver Lake. 201 campsites, open mid-May/June–Sept./Oct.

12 Glass Butte
Bureau of Land Management
P.O. Box 550
Prineville, OR 97754
(503) 447-4115

Rock hounds collect obsidian from this volcanic cinder cone rising from desert floor. Vegetation consists of juniper, sagebrush, and grasses; deer, pronghorns, small game roam the area.

3,000 acres. Late spring, summer, fall best times. Primitive camping.

13 Hart Mountain National Antelope Refuge
P.O. Box 111
Lakeview, OR 97630
(503) 947-3315

Tableland rising above lake-dappled Warner Valley; sanctuary for pronghorns; also home to sage grouse, bobcats, coyotes, and mule deer.

241,000 acres. Spring, summer, fall best times. Roads may be closed by snow and mud in winter and spring. Primitive camping.

14 John Day Fossil Beds N.M.
420 W. Main St.
John Day, OR 97845
(503) 575-0721

3 units—Sheep Rock, Painted Hills, and Clarno—exhibit plant and animal fossils from the Eocene through the Pleistocene epoch.

14,012 acres. Information at HQ and visitor center in John Day; exhibits, interpretive talks. Food and lodging nearby.

15 John Day River
Bureau of Land Management
P.O. Box 550
Prineville, OR 97754
(503) 447-4115

Scenic river flowing between high basaltic cliffs and past colorful rock formations. Deer and small mammals inhabit this rough, remote area; sage, grass, juniper chief vegetation.

40,000 acres. River high enough to float Apr.–July only. Primitive camping.

16 Klamath Forest N.W.R.
Route 1, Box 74
Tulelake, CA 96134
(916) 667-2231

Flat marsh and upland meadow habitat for Canada geese, sandhill cranes, redheads, and mallards; important nesting and migration area for waterfowl. Pine forest supports diversity of wildlife.

16,376 acres. Open dawn to dusk. Spring, fall best times. Food nearby.

17 Klamath N.F.

see California

18 Lewis and Clark N.W.R.
P.O. Box 566
Cathlamet, WA 98612
(206) 795-3915

Sandbars, tidelands, islands, and open water in Columbia River estuary; wintering site for migrating waterfowl.

35,000 acres. Access by boat. Open dawn to dusk. Spring, winter best times. Food and lodging nearby.

19 Lower Klamath N.W.R.

see California

20 McKay Creek N.W.R.
P.O. Box 239
Umatilla, OR 97882
(503) 922-3232

Borders a reservoir; home in winter to some 10,000 geese and 25,000 ducks.

1,837 acres. Closed first Mon. after state waterfowl season to end of Feb. Spring, fall, winter best times. Food and lodging nearby.

21 Malheur N.F.
139 NE Dayton St.
John Day, OR 97845
(503) 575-1731

Rolling mountains timbered with ponderosa pine and Douglas fir tapering off to sagebrush and juniper at edge of Oregon's high desert. Ghost towns. Small wilderness area.

1,459,422 acres. Information at ranger stations in Hines, John Day, and Prairie City. 225 campsites, open May/June–Oct./Nov. Food and lodging nearby.

22 Malheur N.W.R.
P.O. Box 113
Burns, OR 97720
(503) 493-2323

High desert and wetland, sprinkled with ponds and lakes; home to a wide range of mammals and birds; greater sandhill cranes, trumpeter swans, and cinnamon teal nest in large numbers.

183,000 acres. Open dawn to dusk. Mid-May, Sept.–Oct. best times. Activities restricted by area and season; check with HQ. Food and lodging nearby.

23 Mount Hood N.F.
2955 N.W. Division St.
Gresham, OR 97030
(503) 667-0511

Towering firs lining south bank of Columbia River Gorge; snow-clad Mount Hood; lacy waterfalls; glaciers; hot springs; alpine meadows; Mount Hood Wilderness Area. Heavy visitor use.

1,060,744 acres. Reservations required for Indian Henry group site and accepted for Indian Henry camping area. Information at ranger stations in Barlow, Clackamas, Columbia Gorge, Estacada, Hood River, and Zigzag. 56 rooms; 1,432 campsites, open May–Sept.; food services. Food and lodging nearby.

24 North Umpqua River
Bureau of Land Management
777 NW Garden Valley Blvd.
Roseburg, OR 97470
(503) 672-4491

Scenic river flowing between forested banks east of Roseburg; both smooth and white water; premier steelhead fly-fishing stream; rhododendrons. Highway 138 along north side is a state scenic highway.

7.5 miles. Summer, fall best times. Permits required for white-water rafting; available from Umpqua N.F. Campsites; food services. Food and lodging nearby.

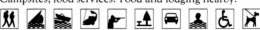

25 Ochoco N.F.
Federal Building
Prineville, OR 97754
(503) 447-6247

Juniper- and pine-covered slopes dovetailing into wide grasslands and semi-arid prairies. Rock formations; streams and lakes. Beaver colonies. Excellent rock-hunting area: agates, rhyolite, jasper.

846,000 acres. Spring, fall best times. Information at ranger stations in Hines, Paulina, and Prineville. 145 campsites, most open Apr./June–Oct., some year round. No drinking water in Big Spring and Ochoco Divide camping areas.

THREE ARCH ROCKS, OREGON

26 Oregon Caves N.M.
19000 Caves Hwy.
Cave Junction, OR 97523
(503) 592-2100

Series of passageways with flowstone formations created by groundwater dissolving marble bedrock. Wildlife watching.

480 acres. Fee for cave tour. Information on OR 46 at exit from OR 199, or call (503) 592-3400. Campfire and interpretive programs in summer only. 29 rooms; food services. Children under 6 not permitted in cave; child care available. Food and lodging nearby.

27 Owyhee River Canyon
Bureau of Land Management
P.O. Box 700
Vale, OR 97918
(503) 473-3144

The Owyhee and its south fork offer exciting white water in a remote high desert setting. Reddish-brown canyons rise up to 1,000 feet above sagebrush-covered slopes at river's edge. Wildlife includes deer, pronghorns, bighorn sheep, Canada geese and other waterfowl.

192 miles of Owyhee; 50 miles of South Fork of Owyhee; part in ID and NV. May 1–June 15 best time; rivers high enough for floating Mar.–June. Ask ahead about requirements and regulations. Information from BLM, Boise District, ID, and Elko District, NV. Primitive camping; food services.

28 Pacific Crest N.S.T.   *see* California

29 Rogue River
Bureau of Land Management
3040 Biddle Rd.
Medford, OR 97504
(503) 776-4173

Designated wild and scenic river flowing through rough terrain in Siskiyou and Coast Ranges. Rogue River N.S.T. parallels river. Hardwood and coniferous forest shelters deer, bears, bobcats, elk, beavers, raccoons, otters, smaller mammals, and birds. Archaeological excavations.

47 miles: 27 recreation area; 20 wild. Spring, fall best times for hiking; summer for white water. White-water boaters limited to 120 a day; 60 assigned to commercial outfitters, 60 determined by lottery held in Mar.; apply in Jan. Rand Visitor Center in recreation area. Primitive camping. Food and lodging nearby.

30 Rogue River N.F.
Federal Building
333 W. 8th St.
P.O. Box 520
Medford, OR 97501
(503) 776-3600

Dense stands of sugar pine and Douglas fir on western slopes of the Cascades. Gorges and canyons; lakes; trout streams; waterfalls; white-water river. Section of Pacific Crest N.S.T.

638,081 acres, part in CA. Visitor center at Union Creek Campground. 30 rooms; 600 campsites, most open May/July–mid-Sept., some year round; food services. No drinking water in some camping areas. Food and lodging nearby.

31 **Siskiyou N.F.**
Box 440
Grants Pass, OR
97526
(503) 479-5301

Dense pine and fir forest with many natural and recreational attractions; Wild and Scenic Rogue, outstanding white-water and fishing river; rare trees and other plants; Kalmiopsis Wilderness.

1,083,000 acres, part in CA. Information at ranger stations in Brookings, Cave Junction, Gold Beach, Grants Pass, and Powers. 268 campsites, most open May–Sept. Food and lodging nearby.

32 **Siuslaw N.F.**
Box 1148
Corvallis, OR 97339
(503) 757-4480

Productive coniferous forest of spruce, hemlock, cedar, and Douglas fir in Coast Range. Includes Oregon Dunes N.R.A.—40 miles of giant coastal sand dunes.

630,000 acres. Cape Perpetua Visitor Center. 950 campsites, some year-round. Food and lodging nearby.

33 **Steens Mountain Recreation Lands**
Bureau of Land Management
74 S. Alvord St.
Burns, OR 97720
(503) 573-5241

Rugged mountains, deep canyons, and isolated plateaus 60 miles south of Burns; home to mule deer, pronghorns, and bighorn sheep.

193,856 acres. Aug. best time. Main access road closed by snow Oct.–mid-July. 39 campsites. Food and lodging nearby.

34 **Umatilla N.F.**
2517 S.W. Hailey Ave.
Pendleton, OR 97801
(503) 276-3811

Mountains with mixed stands of lodgepole and ponderosa pine and grand fir broken by open areas. Valleys, canyons; hot sulfur springs; trout streams; white-water rivers; lush grazing lands; wilderness area. Elk, mule deer.

1,399,342 acres, part in WA. Late June–mid-Nov. best time. Permits required to enter wilderness area. Information at supervisor's office in Pendleton and at ranger stations in Dale, Heppner, and Ukiah, OR, and Pomeroy and Walla Walla, WA. 283 campsites; food services in ski season. Winter sports area. Food nearby.

35 **Umatilla N.W.R.**
P.O. Box 239
Umatilla, OR 97882
(503) 922-3232

Desert with grasslands dotted with marshes and lakes. Ducks, Canada geese, other waterfowl thrive; long-billed curlews nest here; birds of prey; coyotes, mule deer.

22,885 acres, part in WA. Winter best time. Photo blind available. Food and lodging nearby.

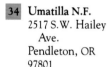

36 Umpqua N.F.
2900 N.W. Stewart
  Pkwy.
Roseburg, OR 97470
(503) 672-6601

Dense coniferous forest on western slopes of the Cascades. Fishing rivers and lakes; cataracts and lacy waterfalls.

989,144 acres. Information at Diamond Lake. 696 campsites, most open May/June–Oct., some year round; food services. Food and lodging nearby.

37 Upper Klamath N.W.R.
Route 1, Box 74
Tulelake, CA 96134
(916) 667-2231

Mainly water and marsh attracting red-necked grebes and other water birds.

14,886 acres. Access by boat. Open dawn to dusk. Spring, summer, fall best times. Food and lodging nearby.

**38 Valley of the
    Giants
    Natural Area**
Bureau of Land
  Management
1717 Fabry Rd.
  SE
P.O. Box 3227
Salem, OR 97302
(503) 399-5643

Remote hillside area with some of the largest old-growth Douglas firs remaining in Oregon. North Fork of the Siletz River traverses area; good steelhead fishing. Elk, owls, woodpeckers, flying squirrels, other animals in forest.

47 acres. Summer best time. 1-mile hike from nearest access road; access roads may be closed by water in winter and spring.

**39 Wallowa-
    Whitman N.F.**
Federal Office Bldg.
P.O. Box 907
Baker, OR 97814
(503) 523-6391

2 forests managed as single unit. Alpine fir and spruce blanket snowcapped mountains. Lakes, glaciers, alpine meadows, granite peaks, canyons; rare wildlife and wild flowers. Eagle Cap Wilderness and Hells Canyon N.R.A.

2,250,900 acres. Spring, summer, fall best times. Information at ranger stations in Baker, Enterprise, Halfway, Joseph, La Grande, Union, and Unity. 1,075 campsites, open May/June–Sept./Oct./Nov. No drinking water in some camping areas. Winter sports area. Food and lodging nearby.

Whitman N.F.   *see* **Wallowa-Whitman N.F.**

40 Willamette N.F.
211 E. 7th Ave.
Eugene, OR 97401
(503) 687-6521

Working forest of Douglas fir. Snowcapped peaks; volcanic formations, lava beds; 350 lakes; waterfalls, hot springs. Includes large parts of 4 wilderness areas.

1,675,373 acres. Reservations required for group campgrounds. Information at ranger stations in Blue River, Detroit, Lowell, McKenzie Bridge, Oakridge, Sweet Home, and Rigdon. 1,346 campsites, some open year round. Food and lodging nearby.

**41 William L.
Finley N.W.R.**
Route 2, Box 208
Corvallis, OR 97333
(503) 757-7236

Winter sanctuary for dusky Canada geese; marsh hawks, kestrels, and red-tailed hawks year round; migrators such as Swainson's and varied thrushes and tundra swans. Three Arch Rocks is sub-unit of refuge.

5,325 acres. Open daylight hours; goose habitat closed Nov. 1–Apr. 15. Spring, fall, winter best times. Information kiosks. Food and lodging nearby.

42 Winema N.F.
P.O. Box 1390
Klamath Falls, OR
97601
(503) 883-6714

Dense pine woods amid peaks and lakes of southern Oregon Cascades; volcanic cone; includes rugged Mountain Lakes Wilderness and Sky Lakes proposed wilderness. Numerous waterfowl.

1,037,690 acres. Summer, winter best times. Information at ranger stations in Chemult, Chiloquin, and Klamath Falls. 50 rooms; 304 campsites, open June–Oct.; food services. Food and lodging nearby.

**43 Yaquina Head
Natural Area**
Bureau of Land
Management
1717 Fabry Rd. SE
P.O. Box 3227
Salem, OR 97302
(503) 399-5643

Scenic headland on northwest coast. Harbor seals and sea lions sun themselves on rocks near beach; colonies of marine birds nest on offshore islands, a designated wilderness area. Key area for watching migrating gray whales in spring and fall. Tide pools.

100 acres. Summer best time. Food and lodging nearby.

Pennsylvania

The famed Delaware Water Gap, a forested canyon threaded by the Delaware River, is the focus of a national recreation area favored by hikers, birders, and canoeists. Tinicum environmental center preserves a patch of tranquillity less than a mile from the runways of Philadelphia International Airport.

1 Allegheny N.F.
222 Liberty St.
P.O. Box 847
Warren, PA 16365
(814) 723-5150

Hardwood forest sweeping across rolling hills. Virgin stands; varied wildlife; brilliant fall foliage. Outstanding recreational opportunities.

510,500 acres. Fall color peaks in mid-Oct.; mountain laurel early to mid-June. User fee. Kinzua Point Information Center open June–Aug. 731 campsites, open April/May–Oct./Nov./Dec.; food services. No drinking water in some camping areas during off season. Food and lodging nearby.

2 Appalachian N.S.T.

see Maine

3 Delaware Water Gap N.R.A.
Bushkill, PA 18324
(717) 588-6637

Scenic area straddles the Delaware River and includes 20 miles of the Appalachian N.S.T. Winter sports such as ice skating and ice fishing. Wildlife watching.

51,000 acres, part in NJ. Kittatinny Point Information Station open daily, May–Oct., less often at other times; Dingmans Falls Visitor Center open late April–Oct.; craft demonstrations, interpretive exhibits. Food and lodging nearby.

4 **Erie N.W.R.**
R.D. 1
Wood Duck La.
Guys Mills, PA
16327
(814) 789-3585

2 pond-speckled units, one with more upland, one with more timbered swampland. White-tailed deer and beavers; waterfowl in spring and fall; nesting warblers; birds of prey.

7,994 acres. Open dawn to dusk. Spring, fall best times. Food and lodging nearby.

5 **Tinicum National Environmental Center**
86th St. and
  Lindbergh Blvd.
Philadelphia, PA
19153
(215) 365-3118

Located in an industrial and residential area of southwest Philadelphia, Tinicum Marsh is the last remaining freshwater tidal wetland in the state. 280 species of birds as well as native mammals and reptiles.

1,200 acres. Open dawn to dusk. Spring, fall best times. Visitor center: guided walks; environmental education resources for schools. Trails, observation platform, and blind. Food and lodging nearby.

Rhode Island

Rhode Island's small and charming coastal refuges protect many kinds of waterfowl and shorebirds. Nature trails wind through old fields and orchards to Trustom Pond, a haven for swans in summer.

1 **Block Island N.W.R.**
Box 307
Charlestown, RI
02813
(401) 364-3106

Northern tip of Block Island, where terns, gulls, piping plovers, and spotted sandpipers nest; large numbers of migrating shorebirds, waterfowl, and songbirds in spring and fall.

29 acres. Open dawn to dusk. Spring, fall best times. Food and lodging nearby.

2 Ninigret N.W.R.
Box 307
Charlestown, RI
02813
(401) 364-3106

Grasslands, scrublands, freshwater ponds, saltwater marsh, and barrier beach. Birding especially good in spring and fall; only place in state where yellow-breasted chats nest.

404 acres. Open dawn to dusk. Spring, fall best times. Food and lodging nearby.

3 Sachuest Point N.W.R.
Box 307
Charlestown, RI
02813
(401) 364-3106

Lush peninsula with a broad range of birdlife, including herons, hawks, swallows, and shorebirds; quail and pheasants frequent upland areas.

228 acres. Open dawn to dusk. Spring, fall best times. Visitor center open May–Sept. Refuge address May–Sept.: P. O. Box 4062, Middletown, RI 02840-0010; (401) 847-5511. Food and lodging nearby.

4 Trustom Pond N.W.R.
Box 307
Charlestown, RI
02813
(401) 364-3106

Brackish pond encircled by upland brush, alfalfa fields, and barrier beach; wintering flocks of Canada, snow, and brant geese; gadwall, black, mallard, and other ducks; cormorants, egrets, and ospreys; shorebird migration site in spring and fall.

579 acres. Open dawn to dusk. Spring, fall best times. Food and lodging nearby.

South Carolina

Sandy beaches, salt marshes, and barrier islands distinguish several federally owned areas here. Among them, coastal Cape Romain National Wildlife Refuge holds an impressive variety of plant and animal species. Francis Marion National Forest takes its name from the Revolutionary War general who operated from the cover of its dusky, moss-hung swamplands.

1 Cape Romain N.W.R.
Route 1, Box 191
Awendaw, SC 29429
(803) 928-3368

Open water, beaches, and salt marsh; timbered upland with marshes and ponds. Nesting site for waders such as snowy egrets and white and glossy ibises; wintering waterfowl; white-tailed deer and alligators.

34,229 acres. Open dawn to dusk. Spring, fall, winter best times. Photo blind available. Food and lodging nearby.

2 Carolina Sandhills N.W.R.
Route 2, Box 130
McBee, SC 29101
(803) 335-8401

Region of sandhills and stands of aged pines, dotted with some 30 lakes. Red-cockaded woodpeckers thrive here; also Pine Barrens tree frogs; waterfowl in winter.

45,591 acres. Open dawn to dusk. Spring, summer, winter best times. Diplay at Lake Bee on visitors' drive. Photo blind available. Food and lodging nearby.

3 Congaree Swamp N.M.
P.O. Box 11938
Columbia, SC 29211
(803) 765-5571

Last significant stand of unspoiled river-bottom hardwoods in southeastern U. S. is preserved here on alluvial floodplain of Congaree River, 20 miles southeast of Columbia.

15,135 acres. Reservations required for guided hikes on Sat. and guided canoe tours on Sun.

4 **Francis Marion N.F.**
P.O. Box 2227
Columbia, SC 29202
(803) 765-5222

Dense coastal swamp with cypress and gum trees draped in Spanish moss; oak, pine, dogwood, redbud. Alligators. Colonial plantations; Revolutionary War sites; old churches, graveyards. Bird watching.

250,000 acres. Spring best time for flower displays. Information at ranger stations in McClellanville and Moncks Corner. 27 campsites; also primitive camping. Food and lodging nearby.

5 **Santee N.W.R.**
Route 2, Box 66
Summerton, SC 29148
(803) 478-2217

Marsh, woods, and upland surrounding a reservoir; southernmost point for wintering Canada geese; home to great numbers of egrets and herons; alligators.

15,095 acres. Open dawn to dusk. Spring, fall, winter best times. Visitor center at junction of I-95 and 301/15. Food and lodging nearby.

6 **Savannah N.W.R.**

see Georgia

7 **Sumter N.F.**
P.O. Box 2227
Columbia, SC 29202
(803) 765-5222

3 distinct areas: mountains covered with pine, hardwood, dogwood, redbud; river bottoms with ancient birch, maple, beech; piedmont with young pine stands, flowering shrubs. Chattooga Wild and Scenic River offers some of the most challenging white water in the East.

360,000 acres. Spring, fall best times for foliage displays. Information at ranger stations in Edgefield, Greenwood, Newberry, Union, and Walhalla. Campsites, some year-round. Food and lodging nearby.

      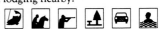

SAVANNAH NATIONAL WILDLIFE REFUGE, SOUTH CAROLINA

South Dakota

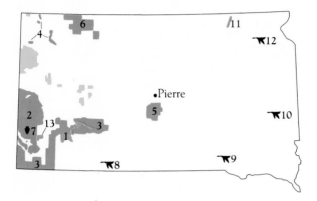

Amid the horizon-stretching Great Plains rise the raw and rugged landforms of Badlands National Park. Natural sculpting has created mazes of caverns glistening with calcite crystals at Wind Cave National Park and Jewel Cave National Monument. Magnificent trumpeter swans, white pelicans, and bald eagles frequent South Dakota's wildlife refuges.

1 Badlands N.P.
P.O. Box 6
Interior, SD 57750
(605) 433-5361

Fossils of animals that lived 25–38 million years ago contrast with abundant wildlife of prairie grasslands; bison, bighorn sheep, deer, pronghorns, and prairie dogs. Sage Creek Wilderness Area.

243,302 acres. Spring, summer, fall best times; winter blizzards may block roads. Entrance fee; reservations required for group camping. Cedar Pass and White River visitor centers: nature walks, evening programs. 20 cabins; 119 campsites; food services. Food and lodging nearby.

2 Black Hills N.F.
P.O. Box 792
Custer, SD 57730
(605) 673-2251

Thick mantle of evergreens covers mountain range capped by craggy pinnacles. Lakes, creeks, waterfalls; deep canyons; meadows; geologic formations. Historic gold rush and cowboy area. Mount Rushmore National Memorial.

1,235,453 acres, part in WY. Visitor center at Pactola Reservoir open Memorial Day–Labor Day; information also at ranger stations in Custer, Deadwood, Hill City, Rapid City, and Spearfish, South Dakota; New Castle and Sundance, Wyoming. Rooms; 702 campsites, open May/June–Sept./Oct./Nov.; food services. Winter sports area. Food and lodging nearby.

3 **Buffalo Gap N.G.**
P.O. Box 425
Wall, SD 57790
(605) 279-2125

Rolling prairie with mixed shortgrass and tallgrass, some shrubs; surrounds Badlands N.P. Wildlife includes deer, pronghorns, coyotes, foxes. Many areas for rock hunting.

591,771 acres. Late May–early June, Sept.–Oct. best times. 5 campsites. No established backpacking or hiking trails. Food and lodging nearby.

4 **Custer N.F.**

see Montana

5 **Fort Pierre N.G.**
P.O. Box 417
Pierre, SD 57501
(605) 224-5517

Gently rolling, treeless prairie. More than 200 species of birds have been spotted, including songbirds, waterfowl, birds of prey, and greater prairie-chickens.

115,996 acres. June, Sept.–Oct. best times. All off-road travel prohibited Sept.–Nov. Food and lodging nearby.

6 **Grand River N.G.**
Grand River Ranger
District
P.O. Box 390
Lemmon, SD 57638
(605) 374-3592

Rolling shortgrass and midgrass prairie; some badland areas. Wildlife includes deer, pronghorns, prairie dogs, red foxes, coyotes, birds of prey, Canada geese and other waterfowl.

156,000 acres. Interior inaccessible by passenger car. June, Sept.–Oct. best times. Food and lodging nearby.

  more icons

7 **Jewel Cave N.M.**
Custer, SD 57730
(605) 673-2288

Series of limestone caves connected by narrow corridors; numerous side galleries; calcite crystal encrustations and other mineral formations.

1,275 acres. Cave tour daily, May–Sept.; less often rest of year. Fees for guided tours; reservations accepted for spelunking and group historic tours. Visitor center: interpretive exhibits. Food and lodging nearby.

8 **Lacreek N.W.R.**
Star Route 3, Box 14
Martin, SD 57551
(605) 685-6508

Grasslands and marsh bordering the Nebraska sandhills; nesting site for white pelicans and trumpeter swans; other birds include Canada geese, blue-winged teal, mallards, upland birdlife.

16,250 acres. Open dawn to dusk. Campsites. Food and lodging nearby.

**9 Lake Andes
N.W.R.**
Rural Route 1
Box 77
Lake Andes, SD
57356
(605) 487-7603

Mixed habitat of marsh, timberland, prairie, and ponds; huge numbers of Canada geese, mallards, pintails, wigeons, green-winged teal, and other waterfowl.

5,942 acres. Open dawn to dusk. Owens Bay Nature Trail and Picnic Area open Apr. 15–Oct. 15. Spring, fall best times. Food and lodging nearby.

**10 Madison
W.M.D.**
Box 48
Madison, SD 57042
(605) 256-2974

Wetlands comprising 200 waterfowl production areas; ducks and other wildlife.

25,000 acres. Open 8 a.m.–4:30 p.m. Spring, fall best times. Food and lodging nearby.

**11 Sand Lake
N.W.R.**
Rural Route 1
Columbia, SD 57433
(605) 885-6320

Prairie and woods alongside marshland and lakes that attract enormous flocks of waterfowl; in spring and fall, white and blue snow geese may total 300,000, with a comparable number of ducks. Other visitors include white pelicans, black and white western grebes, and 7 hawk species; white-tailed deer and red foxes also common.

21,451 acres. Open dawn to dusk. Spring, summer, fall best times. Information booth on Hwy. 10. Food and lodging nearby.

12 Waubay N.W.R.
Rural Route 1
Box 79
Waubay, SD 57273
(605) 947-4695

Marsh, woods, and upland dotted with some two dozen lakes and ponds. Nesting birds such as western and red-necked grebes and many species of waterfowl, including Canada geese; abundant white-tailed deer.

4,650 acres. Open dawn to dusk. Spring, fall best times. Food and lodging nearby.

13 Wind Cave N.P.
Hot Springs, SD
57747
(605) 745-4600

Limestone cavern in the Black Hills, with intricate formations of boxwork and calcite crystal. Wildlife includes bison, elk, deer, prairie dogs, pronghorns.

28,056 acres. Summer, fall best times. Cave tours daily; limited schedule in winter; tour fee. Visitor center: candlelight and spelunking tours; evening campfire programs; interpretive exhibits. 100 campsites; food services in summer. Food and lodging nearby.

Tennessee

In eastern Tennessee, Great Smoky Mountains National Park overlaps part of the Appalachian's highest range. June brings rhododendrons into brilliant bloom here and in Cherokee National Forest. Big South Fork National River meanders north through scenic gorges into Kentucky. Tennessee's five national wildlife refuges cluster in lowlands and woodlands to the west.

1 **Appalachian N.S.T.**   *see* Maine

2 **Big South Fork
   N.R. and N.R.A.**
P.O. Drawer 630
Oneida, TN 37841
(615) 569-6389

Scenic river valley of the free-flowing Big South Fork of the Cumberland River and its tributaries; notable natural and historical features.

122,960 acres, part in KY. Spring, fall best times. Campground expected to open in 1985. Food and lodging nearby.

3 **Cherokee N.F.**
2800 N. Ocoee St.
P.O. Box 2010
Cleveland, TN
37311
(615) 476-9700

Dense stands of mixed pine and hardwood in rugged mountain backcountry; virgin timber; flowering rhododendron and mountain laurel. Spring and fall displays. Wildlife includes Russian boars.

625,000 acres. Information at ranger stations in Benton, Elizabethton, Erwin, Etowah, Greenville, and Tellico Plains. 686 campsites, many year-round. No drinking water in Low Gap camping area. Food and lodging nearby.

4 **Cross Creeks
   N.W.R.**
Route 1, Box 229
Dover, TN 37058
(615) 232-7477

Fertile lowland bounded by hills and steep, stony bluffs. Waterfowl abound in winter, chiefly Canada geese and mallards; golden and bald eagles also winter here; various hawks may be seen year round.

8,862 acres. Open dawn to dusk. Dec.–Jan., Mar.–Apr. best times. Food and lodging nearby.

5 **Cumberland Gap
   N.H.P.**

see Kentucky

GREAT SMOKY MOUNTAINS NATIONAL PARK, TENNESSEE

6 Great Smoky Mountains N.P.
Gatlinburg, TN 37738
(615) 436-5615

One of the oldest mountain ranges on earth, with some of the highest peaks east of the Black Hills. Plant species distinctive for diversity, abundance, size. Bird watching.

520,004 acres, part in NC. Late Apr.–early May best time for wild flowers and migrating birds; June–July for rhododendrons; Oct. for brilliant foliage. Camping permits required; reservations accepted for 3 developed campgrounds May–Oct. Information at park HQ and visitor center; interpretive programs. Rooms; 1,017 campsites; food services June–Oct. Food and lodging nearby.

7 Hatchie N.W.R.
Box 187
Brownsville, TN 38012
(901) 772-0501

Timbered lowland laced with streams and dotted with lakes alongside fertile upland. More than 200 bird species, including shorebirds, marsh and water birds, waterfowl, birds of prey, songbirds, wild turkeys; deer, raccoons, rabbits.

11,556 acres. Open dawn to dusk. Spring, summer, fall best times. Motor vehicles prohibited in fields and woods and on roads and trails marked "closed." Food and lodging nearby.

8 Lower Hatchie N.W.R.
Box 187
Brownsville, TN 38012
(901) 772-0501

Bottomland hardwoods; seasonally flooded flats of oak and hickory cut by permanent sloughs and cypress-tupelo swamps. Abundant wildlife includes wood ducks, mallards, white-tailed deer, wild turkeys, swamp rabbits, and a variety of songbirds and wading birds.

1,990 acres. Sept.–Dec. best time. Entire area deeply flooded Jan.–May. Food and lodging nearby.

9 Reelfoot N.W.R.
Route 2
Union City, TN 38261
(901) 538-2481

Reelfoot Lake, its basin formed by an earthquake and filled by the waters of the Mississippi; giant cypresses loom above shoal inlets. Ducks and geese; 56 fish species; numerous bald eagles in winter. Lake Isom is sub-unit of refuge.

10,142 acres, part in KY. Open dawn to dusk. Fall, winter best times. Some roads occasionally closed to provide wintering waterfowl sanctuary. Food and lodging nearby.

10 Tennessee N.W.R.
Box 849
Paris, TN 38242
(901) 642-2091

Woodlands and farm plots bordering Kentucky Lake. Golden and bald eagles and great flocks of ducks and Canada geese winter here; quail and white-tailed deer.

51,358 acres. Open dawn to dusk. Spring, fall best times. 15 campsites; food services. Photo blind available. Food and lodging nearby.

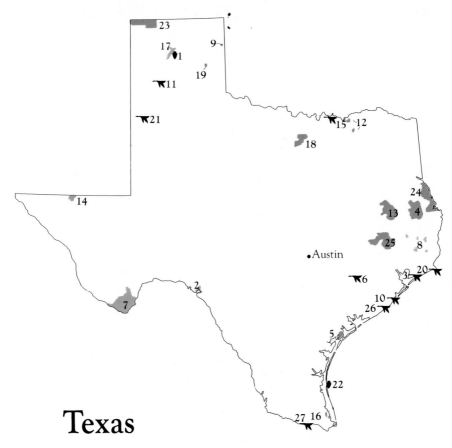

Texas

Variety marks the federal lands of the second largest state. Big Bend boasts wilderness scenery and desert ecology, and Guadalupe Mountains National Park contains parts of an immense fossil reef, formed more than 200 million years ago. Padre Island National Seashore promises some relief from inland summer heat, as do reservoirs and lakes in national recreation areas and forests—the latter all within a relatively small area in east Texas. Nearby, the 20 species of wild orchid that thrive at Big Thicket National Preserve represent only a tiny sampling of the myriad plant types found there.

1 **Alibates Flint Quarries N.M.**
c/o Lake Meredith N.R.A.
P.O. Box 1438
Fritch, TX 79036
(806) 857-3151

For more than 10,000 years, pre-Columbian Indians quarried flint here to make implements such as knives, scrapers, and points.

1,333 acres. Tours at 10 a.m. and 2 p.m. in summer; off-season tours by appointment only; call (806) 857-3152. Bates Canyon Information Station at Lake Meredith. Food and lodging nearby.

2 Amistad N.R.A.
Star Route 2
Box 5-P
Hwy. 90 W.
Del Rio, TX 78840
(512) 775-7491

Enormous clear-water reservoir on the Rio Grande, joint project of U. S. and Mexico; surrounded by desert and rugged mountains. Water sports and swimming 9 months of the year.

62,452 acres. Open daylight hours. Reservations necessary for group camping and special events. Visitor center in Del Rio; Amistad Visitor Center open in summer. 50 campsites. Food and lodging nearby.

3 Anahuac N.W.R.
Box 278
Anahuac, TX 77514
(409) 267-3337

Wetland and saltwater ponds along Gulf of Mexico. As many as 20 kinds of ducks and 4 species of geese visit Oct.–Mar.; water birds such as herons, egrets, and ibises; alligators abundant, especially at Shoveler Pond; muskrats and nutria common.

24,293 acres. Spring, winter best times. Campsites. No drinking water on refuge. Food and lodging nearby.

4 Angelina N.F.
1907 Atkinson Dr.
Lufkin, TX 75901
(409) 634-7709

Hills covered with dense stands of longleaf pine and hardwood. Fishing rivers, lakes; wild flowers. Waterskiing on Sam Rayburn Reservoir.

155,000 acres. Swimming fee. Information at ranger station in Lufkin. 240 campsites, some open year round, others Mar.–Oct.; food services. Food and lodging nearby.

5 Aransas N.W.R.
Box 100
Austwell, TX 77950
(512) 286-3559

Gulf Coast refuge where extremely rare whooping cranes winter; some 350 species of birds counted, among them sandhill cranes, wood storks, and roseate spoonbills; white-tailed deer.

54,000 acres. Open dawn to dusk. Spring, fall, winter best times. Wildlife interpretive center. Observation tower with wheelchair ramp. Food nearby.

6 Attwater Prairie Chicken N.W.R.
Box 518
Eagle Lake, TX 77434
(713) 234-3021

Tallgrass prairie set aside to protect Attwater's prairie-chickens, usually numbering just over 150; in winter, white-tailed hawks, caracaras, vesper and Le Conte's sparrows, waterfowl.

8,000 acres. Open dawn to dusk. Fall, winter best times. Reservations required for photo blinds Feb. 1–Apr. 15. Food and lodging nearby.

7 Big Bend N.P.
Big Bend National
Park, TX 79834
(915) 477-2251

Rugged, isolated horseshoe bend in the Rio Grande. 61 varieties of cactus; rare drooping junipers; 400 bird species, including Colima warblers; Carmen white-tailed deer, badgers, javelinas. Summer temperatures 100°F and above.

740,118 acres. Permits required for backcountry camping and for boating on Rio Grande. Information at park HQ; interpretive exhibits. 33 rooms; 190 campsites; food services.

8 Big Thicket National Preserve
P.O. Box 7408
Beaumont, TX 77706
(409) 839-2689

Diverse region of bayous, forests, and uplands. Plant species of north, south, and west in close proximity.

84,550 acres. Spring, fall best times. Permits required for backcountry use. Information at temporary HQ; visitor station. Limited facilities. Food and lodging nearby.

9 Black Kettle N.G.

see Oklahoma

10 Brazoria N.W.R.
1208 N. Velasco
Box 1088
Angleton, TX 77515
(409) 849-6062

Salt marsh bordering coastal prairie attracts great flocks of ducks and geese as well as wood storks and roseate spoonbills; alligators also common.

10,361 acres. Access by boat. Open dawn to dusk. Spring, fall, winter best times. Food and lodging nearby.

11 Buffalo Lake N.W.R.
Box 228
Umbarger, TX 79091
(806) 499-3382

When full in years of good rainfall, lake may attract 250,000 ducks and 80,000 geese in spring and autumn. Numerous birds of prey, several thousand prairie dogs, and a herd of mule deer are permanent residents here.

7,664 acres. Winter best time. Information at Muleshoe N.W.R. 10 campsites. Food and lodging nearby.

12 Caddo N.G.
P.O. Box 507
Decatur, TX 76234
(817) 627-5475

Rolling hills with mixed grassland and wooded areas. Wildlife includes deer, bobwhite quail, bobcats, coyotes.

17,796 acres. Spring, summer, fall best times. Vehicle travel restricted to designated roads. 1 cabin and several rooms at lodge. Food and lodging nearby.

13 Davy Crockett N.F.
Neches Ranger District
East Loop 304
Crockett, TX 75835
(409) 544-2046

Shortleaf and loblolly pine areas, with mixed hardwoods in Neches and Trinity river basins. Wildlife management area in forest. Catfish and bass fishing in rivers and lakes; deer, squirrels, quail, and doves.

161,497 acres. Swimming fee. Information at ranger stations in Apple Springs and Crockett. 70 campsites, some year-round; food services.

14 Guadalupe Mountains N.P.
3225 National Parks Hwy.
Carlsbad, NM 88220
(915) 828-3385

Rugged mountain mass with geologic features such as Permian-age fossil reefs, a major fault, deep canyons. 80 miles of hiking trails. Frijole and Williams Ranch historic sites; ruins of Butterfield Overland Mail stage station.

76,293 acres. Fall best time. McKittrick Canyon open daylight hours only. Permits required for overnight backcountry trips. Frijole Information Station: guided tours and evening programs in summer. 54 campsites.

15 Hagerman N.W.R.
Route 3, Box 123
Sherman, TX 75090
(214) 786-2826

Water, marsh, and upland peppered with working oil wells. Common visitors include Canada geese, white pelicans, and some dozen species of ducks; shorebirds such as Baird's sandpipers and dowitchers appear seasonally; roadrunners and scissor-tailed flycatchers common in summer.

11,319 acres. Open dawn to dusk. Spring, fall, winter best times. Information at local chambers of commerce. Food and lodging nearby.

16 Laguna Atascosa N.W.R.
Box 450
Rio Hondo, TX 78583
(512) 748-3607

Once part of a delta of the Rio Grande. Bobcats, ocelots, and abundant white-tailed deer; birdlife includes black-bellied whistling ducks, Canada and snow geese, green jays, and chachalacas.

45,204 acres. Open dawn to dusk. Fall, winter best times.

17 Lake Meredith N.R.A.
P.O. Box 1438
Fritch, TX 79036
(806) 857-3151

Artificial lake on the Canadian River. Water sports include waterskiing and scuba diving.

44,951 acres. Many areas closed in winter. Information at HQ in Fritch; interpretive exhibits. Campsites; food services. Food and lodging nearby.

18 Lyndon B. Johnson N.G.
P.O. Box 507
Decatur, TX 76234
(817) 627-5475

Flat grasslands interspersed with wooded areas. Wildlife includes deer, bobwhite quail, bobcats, and coyotes.

20,320 acres. Summer best time. Vehicle travel restricted to designated roads. 3 campsites. Food and lodging nearby.

19 McClellan Creek N.G.
P.O. Box 266
Cheyenne, OK 73628
(405) 497-2143

Rolling hills with midgrass to tallgrass prairie and some timber. Wildlife includes deer, wild turkeys, bobwhite quail. Lake McClellan is the major recreation area; waterskiing.

1,449 acres. Sept.–Oct. best time. User fee. 51 campsites; food services. Food nearby.

BIG BEND NATIONAL PARK, TEXAS

20 **McFaddin and Texas Point N.W.R.**
Box 278
Anahuac, TX 77514
(409) 267-3337

Marshland on upper Texas coast, important to wintering migratory waterfowl in the Central flyway. More than 60,000 snow geese; 23 species of ducks numbering up to 100,000. McFaddin Marsh has dense population of alligators. Also various mammals.

50,654 acres. Spring, winter best times. Information at Anahuac N.W.R. Campsites. Food and lodging nearby.

21 **Muleshoe N.W.R.**
Box 549
Muleshoe, TX 79347
(806) 946-3341

Grass-coated sandhills dappled with lakes that attract enormous flocks of sandhill cranes in fall and winter; geese and ducks thrive when water is available, as do wood warblers and other songbirds.

5,809 acres. Spring, fall, winter best times. 8 campsites.

22 **Padre Island N.S.**
9405 S. Padre Island Dr.
Corpus Christi, TX 78418
(512) 937-2621

Barrier island with wide sand beaches stretching 80 miles along Gulf Coast. Surfing, snorkeling, scuba and skin diving, waterskiing; shell collecting; wildlife watching.

133,919 acres. Fall best time. Malaquite Visitor Center: interpretive exhibits and programs. Chartered fishing trips. 150 campsites; food services. Food and lodging nearby.

23 **Rita Blanca N.G.**
Box 38
Texline, TX 79807
(806) 362-4254

Rolling shortgrass to midgrass prairie. Wildlife includes pronghorns, prairie dogs, pheasants, quail, and many non-game birds.

77,413 acres, part in OK. Open May–Oct. June best time. Food and lodging nearby.

24 **Sabine N.F.**
Tenaha Ranger District
101 S. Bolivar
San Augustine, TX 75972
(409) 275-2634

Rolling clay and sand hills near the Texas-Louisiana border, mantled with southern pine and hardwoods. Fishing rivers; large reservoir.

188,220 acres. Swimming fee. Information at ranger stations in Hemphill and San Augustine. 246 campsites, most open Mar. 1–Oct. 1. Food and lodging nearby.

25 **Sam Houston N.F.**
San Jacinto Ranger District
407 N. Belcher
Cleveland, TX 77327
(713) 592-6462

Thick woods of shortleaf and loblolly pines with mixed hardwoods. Numerous lakes and small streams; wild flowers. Section of 140-mile hiking trail; Big Creek Scenic Area. Waterskiing.

160,453 acres. Swimming fee. Information at ranger stations in Cleveland and New Waverly. 88 campsites, most year-round; food services. Food and lodging nearby.

26 **San Bernard**
N.W.R.
Box 1088
Angleton, TX 77515
(409) 849-6062

Coastal salt marsh around Cowtrap Lakes is ancestral wintering ground of large flocks of snow geese; marsh birds abundant year round.

24,454 acres. Open dawn to dusk. Spring, fall, winter best times. Food and lodging nearby.

27 **Santa Ana N.W.R.**
Route 1, Box 202A
Alamo, TX 78516
(512) 787-3079

Preserves area where subtropical and temperate life zones meet. Largest single tract of native subtropical vegetation remaining in south Texas. Home to such birds as Altamira orioles, least grebes, chachalacas, red-billed pigeons, black-shouldered kites, tropical kingbirds, and green jays.

2,080 acres. Open dawn to dusk. Spring, fall, winter best times. Private cars allowed on tour road Apr.–Nov., 9 a.m.–4:30 p.m.; tram operated Fri.–Mon., Dec.–Mar. Photo blinds available. Food and lodging nearby.

Texas Point
N.W.R.

see **McFaddin and Texas Point N.W.R.**

Utah

Towering spires and pinnacles, graceful arches and natural bridges, colorful cliffs and gorges: Ten national park system areas preserve the unique geologic spectacle of southern Utah. Lake Powell offers 1,900 miles of mid-desert shoreline and cooling Colorado River waters behind Glen Canyon Dam. Of the federal areas that comprise almost two-thirds of Utah, the lion's share goes to BLM districts and then to forests dotted with acclaimed ski resorts. Tundra swans—the largest numbers anywhere—and millions of other migrating birds congregate at Bear River wildlife refuge.

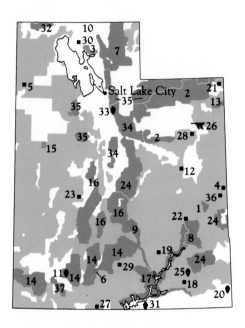

1 **Arches N.P.**
446 S. Main St.
Moab, UT 84532
(801) 259-7164

Colorful red-rock country with sandstone arches shaped by erosion. Delicate Arch; Landscape Arch, earth's longest natural span—291 feet. Wildlife watching. Summer temperatures reach 110°F.

73,379 acres. Spring, fall best times; mid-May for wild flowers. Entrance fee; permits required for backcountry use; reservations required for group campsites. Visitor center: interpretive exhibits; walks and talks. 53 campsites. Food and lodging nearby.

2 **Ashley N.F.**
1680 W. Hwy. 40
Suite 1150
Vernal, UT 84078
(801) 789-1181

Dense stands of pine on mountains rising above sagebrush-covered benchland. Scenic gorges; exposed geologic formations a billion years old; fossils; primitive area.

1,385,000 acres, part in WY. Information at ranger stations in Duchesne, Manila, Roosevelt, and Vernal. 1,269 campsites, most open May–Oct. Winter sports area; waterskiing. Food and lodging nearby.

3 **Bear River Migratory Bird Refuge**
Box 459
Brigham City, UT 84302
(801) 744-2201

Salt marsh and shoal ponds where Bear River pours into Great Salt Lake; noted for tremendous variety and number of migrating birds, including marbled godwits, eared grebes, swallows, and tundra swans; also common seasonally are killdeer, coots, and willets.

64,895 acres. Open 8 a.m. to sunset; closed weekends Jan. 1–Mar. 15. Spring, summer, fall best times. Campsites. Food and lodging nearby.

4 **Black Ridge Canyons**

see Colorado

5 **Bonneville Salt Flats**
Bureau of Land Management
2370 S. 2300 W.
Salt Lake City, UT 84119
(801) 524-5348

Vast saline plain, remnant of a Pleistocene lake bed. Site of automobile races since 1914; races held primarily between July 15 and Sept. 30.

30,200 acres. Sept. best time. Flats flooded in fall and winter. Food and lodging nearby.

6 **Bryce Canyon N.P.**
Bryce Canyon, UT 84717
(801) 834-5322

Colorful rock formations carved by erosion along 20 miles of the Pink Cliffs, more than 8,000 feet above sea level. Wildlife watching.

35,835 acres. Entrance fee; permits required for backcountry use and for snowshoeing and overnight camping in winter. Visitor center: slide programs and exhibits; guided walks, campfire talks. 140 rooms; 226 campsites; food services in summer. Food and lodging nearby.

7 **Cache N.F.**
8226 Federal Bldg.
125 S. State St.
Salt Lake City, UT 84138
(801) 524-5042

Land of rugged mountains, stands of aspen, pine, and fir, and lush grazing areas. Limestone caves with stalagmites and stalactites; canyons with marine fossils.

679,104 acres, part in ID. Reservations required for group campsites. Information at ranger stations in Logan and Ogden. 769 campsites, open May/June–Sept./Oct. Food and lodging nearby.

8 Canyonlands
N.P.
446 S. Main St.
Moab, UT 84532
(801) 259-7164

Trails on vertical sandstone cliffs loop precipitously down to Colorado River. Dramatic red sandstone formations. Ancient Indian pictographs. Wildlife watching.

337,570 acres. Fall best time; spring for wild flowers. Park virtually roadless except for miles of jeep trails; jeep rentals available. Permits required for backcountry and float trips; reservations required for group campsites. Visitor center at Arches N.P.: interpretive exhibits. 38 campsites; jeep tours.

9 Capitol Reef
N.P.
Torrey, UT 84775
(801) 425-3871

Nearly all of Waterpocket Fold, a 100-mile-long fold in the earth's surface, lies within the park; deep gorges, towering cliffs. Ancient Indian storage huts and petroglyphs. Extreme summer and winter temperatures.

241,904 acres. Permits required for backcountry use; reservations available for group campsites. Visitor center: interpretive exhibits, slide programs. 54 campsites. Food and lodging nearby.

10 Caribou N.F.

see Idaho

11 Cedar Breaks
N.M.
P.O. Box 749
Cedar City, UT
84720
(801) 586-9451

Gigantic natural amphitheater created by erosion in the Pink Cliffs, whose rocks reveal 47 different shades of pink.

6,155 acres. Road open mid-May through fall, depending on weather. Reservations available for 1 group campsite. Visitor center: interpretive talks, evening program. 30 campsites, none year-round.

12 Desolation and
Gray Canyons of
the Green River
Bureau of Land
Management
P.O. Box AB
Price, UT 84501
(801) 637-4584

Mile-deep gorge explored by geologist John Wesley Powell in 1869; located in uninhabited area north of town of Green River. Habitat for mule deer, bobcats, birds of prey; firs, willows, grasses, and junipers grow here.

84 river miles. Apr.–Oct. best time. Entrance fee; permits required for float trips; apply before Mar. 1. Primitive camping. Food and lodging nearby.

13 Dinosaur N.M.

see Colorado

14 **Dixie N.F.**
82 N. 100 E.
Cedar City, UT
84720
(801) 586-2421

Steep country of colored cliffs, deep canyons, rock formations; lakes and streams. Forested slopes act as watershed. Remnants of historic Spanish Trail.

1,885,000 acres. Fall best time. Reservations available for group camping. Information at ranger stations in Cedar City, Escalante, Panguitch, St. George, and Teasdale. 555 campsites, open May/June–Sept./Oct.; food services. Food and lodging nearby.

15 **Fish Springs N.W.R.**
P.O. Box 568
Dugway, UT 84022
(801) 522-5353

Marshland amid desert, nourished by springs and fronting desert mountains. Summer nesters include avocets, eared grebes, Canada geese, ducks, snowy egrets; among winter visitors are eagles, hawks, swans; coyotes, muskrats also common.

17,992 acres. Open daylight hours. Spring, fall best times. Visitor contact station. Very remote; bring drinking water.

16 **Fishlake N.F.**
115 E. 900 N.
Richfield, UT 84701
(801) 896-4491

Dense stands of spruce, pine, fir, and aspen on upper slopes of high plateaus; sparse growth on middle and lower slopes. Lush grazing meadows; Fish Lake, other lakes and streams; elk, deer.

1,427,000 acres. Reservations accepted for some camping areas. Information at ranger stations in Beaver, Fillmore, Loa, and Richfield. 250 campsites, open May/June–Oct.; food services. Food and lodging nearby.

17 **Glen Canyon N.R.A.**
P.O. Box 1507
Page, AZ 86040
(602) 645-2471

Glen Canyon Dam, 710 feet high, impounds the sparkling waters of the Colorado River in 186-mile-long Lake Powell. Picturesque Escalante Canyon; slickrock sandstone; steep cliffs; narrow canyons. Wildlife includes bald eagles, peregrine falcons, desert bighorn sheep, mountain lions. San Juan River for floating; some white water.

1,245,855 acres, part in AZ. Spring, summer, fall best times. Visitor center by Glen Canyon Dam: dam tours, interpretive exhibits. Lodge; 385 campsites; food services. Food and lodging nearby.

BRYCE CANYON NATIONAL PARK, UTAH

18 Grand Gulch Primitive Area
Bureau of Land Management
P.O. Box 7
Monticello, UT 84532
(801) 587-2201

Anasazi Indian site more than 1,000 years old; remains of cliff dwellings, pottery, and tools. Wildlife includes rabbits, mule deer, bighorn sheep; plants mostly grasses, cactuses, junipers. Extremely hot in summer.

35,000 acres. Mar.–Nov. best time. Permits required. Information at Kane Gulch Ranger Station on U-261, open Apr.–Nov. Primitive camping.

19 Henry Mountains Buffalo Herd
Bureau of Land Management
P.O. Box 99
Hanksville, UT 84734
(801) 542-3461

Peaks more than 11,000 feet high; canyons with many pictographs; visited over the years by explorers, prospectors, and ranchers. Bison roam the area, 60 miles south of Hanksville.

150,000 acres. Spring, fall best times. Permits required for organized events. 15 campsites.

20 Hovenweep N.M.

see Colorado

21 John Jarvie Historic Site
Bureau of Land Management
170 S. 500 E.
Vernal, UT 84078
(801) 789-1362

Frontier setting in Browns Park on Green River; visited by mountain men, cattlemen, and outlaws such as Butch Cassidy and the Sundance Kid. Junipers and desert shrubs; mule deer, pronghorns, wintering bald eagles.

35 acres. Open 8 a.m.–5 p.m. May–Nov. best time.

22 Labyrinth Canyon
Bureau of Land Management
P.O. Box AB
Price, UT 84501
(801) 637-4584

Green River meanders below colorful cliffs; side canyons and trails; geyser; Indian petroglyphs. Wildlife includes coyotes, beavers, herons, egrets, ravens.

70 river miles. Apr.–Oct. best time. Primitive camping. Food and lodging nearby.

23 Little Sahara Recreation Area
Bureau of Land Management
500 N. 15 E.
Fillmore, UT 84631
(801) 743-6801

Giant dunes, juniper-covered hills, and sagebrush flats 115 miles south of Salt Lake City. Wildlife includes lizards, hawks, coyotes. Summer temperatures often reach 100°F.

60,000 acres. Spring, fall best times. Permits required for organized events. Visitor center. 172 campsites. Food and lodging nearby.

24 Manti-LaSal N.F.
599 W. Price River Dr.
Price, UT 84501
(801) 637-2817

4 separated areas. Manti unit: rugged plateau with grasslands and dense woods of aspen, fir, and spruce. LaSal and Blue Mountain units: rugged plateau with volcanic peaks; piñon, juniper, aspen, pine, fir, and spruce. Sanpitch unit: steep, rugged mountains with grassland, piñon, juniper, oakbrush, aspen, and pine.

1,265,254 acres, part in CO. Access may be limited in May and June. Aspens turn in Sept. Reservations required for several camping areas; available at all. Information at ranger stations in Ephraim, Ferron, Moab, Monticello, and Price. 136 campsites, open May/June–Oct. Food and lodging nearby.

25 Natural Bridges N.M.
c/o Canyonlands N.P.
446 S. Main St.
Moab, UT 84532
(801) 259-7165

3 huge sandstone bridges with Hopi Indian names: Owachomo, Kachina, and Sipapu. Sipapu has a span of 268 feet and rises 220 feet above the streambed.

7,779 acres. Late Apr.–Oct. best time; hiking trails closed in winter. Entrance fee. Visitor center: interpretive exhibits. 13 campsites. Do not enter or disturb any of the Indian ruins.

26 Ouray N.W.R.
447 E. Main St.
Suite 4
Vernal, UT 84078
(801) 789-0351

Marsh and desert edging the Green River; many golden and bald eagles in winter and spring; migrating sandhill cranes visit, sometimes with adopted whooping cranes; endangered humpbacked chub and Colorado squawfish.

11,483 acres. Spring, fall best times.

27 Paria Canyon Primitive Area
Bureau of Land Management
P.O. Box 724
1579 N. Main
Cedar City, UT 84720
(801) 586-2401

Red-rock canyon walls tower up to 1,500 feet above shallow river. Side canyons harbor mule deer and mountain lions. Giant natural arch in Wrather Canyon; Indian petroglyphs, sandstone formations in Buckskin Gulch.

27,515 acres, part in AZ. Early spring, fall best times. Beware of flash floods during spring runoff and summer thunderstorms. Register and check water conditions with ranger station at White House entrance; information there and at BLM offices in St. George and Kanab. Primitive camping.

28 Pariette Wetlands
Bureau of Land Management
170 S. 500 E.
Vernal, UT 84078
(801) 789-1362

Designated habitat management area 20 miles southeast of Roosevelt. Wetland nesting and migratory habitat for ducks, geese, shorebirds; habitat for birds of prey such as hawks and falcons; resting site for migrating cranes, eagles.

9,033 acres. Apr.–May, Sept.–Oct. best times. 5 campsites.

29 Phipps-Death Hollow
Bureau of Land Management
P.O. Box 724
1579 N. Main
Cedar City, UT 84720
(801) 586-2401

Rugged red and white sandstone canyonlands. Arches, mesas, plateaus; canyon of the Escalante River and several tributaries; waterfalls. Calf Creek Recreation Area.

34,288 acres. Mar.–Nov. best time. Reservations required for group campsite. 13 campsites; primitive camping. Food and lodging nearby.

30 Railroad Grade
Bureau of Land Management
2370 S. 2300 W.
Salt Lake City, UT 84119
(801) 524-5348

Historic 90-mile stretch of the nation's first transcontinental railroad grade, extending from Lucin to Ogden over Promontory Summit; remains of railroad stations used from 1869 to 1904.

10,000 acres. May–Oct. best time. Site very remote; come fully prepared.

31 Rainbow Bridge N.M.
c/o Glen Canyon N.R.A.
P.O. Box 1507
Page, AZ 86040
(602) 645-2471

With a height of 290 feet and a span of 275 feet, this pink sandstone formation is the world's largest natural bridge. Sacred to the Hopi and Navajo Indians; offerings to the gods used to be placed in canyon below bridge.

160 acres. Access by horse or boat or on foot. Apr.–early June, Sept.–Oct. best times; extremely hot in summer. Information at Glen Canyon N.R.A. Before beginning a trail trip, call Navajo Mountain Trading Post (602-283-5322) about condition of trails, other factors.

32 Sawtooth N.F. and N.R.A.

see Idaho

33 Timpanogos Cave N.M.
Rural Route 3
Box 200
American Fork, UT 84003
(801) 756-5238

Series of 3 limestone caves inside 12,000-foot Mount Timpanogos; branching formations called helictites.

250 acres. Cave open daily May–Sept. depending on weather. Snow and ice make trail to cave impassable from late Oct. through Apr. Cave tour fee; advance reservations requested for groups of 20 or more. Hike and tour take about 3 hours; cave tour only, 1 hour. Visitor center open year round. Food services. Food and lodging nearby.

34 Uinta N.F.
88 West 100 North
Provo, UT 84601
(801) 377-5780

Working timberland and watershed area on mountains rising from desert. Spruce, fir, aspen, maple, and oak; brilliant fall foliage. Deep canyons; waterfalls; caves. Lone Peak Wilderness Area. Heavy summer recreational use.

910,960 acres. Reservations accepted for some group camping areas. Information at ranger stations in Heber City, Pleasant Grove, and Spanish Fork. 614 campsites, most open May/June–Sept./Oct.; gondola to see Bridal Veil Falls. Food and lodging nearby.

35 Wasatch N.F.
8226 Federal Bldg.
125 S. State St.
Salt Lake City, UT
84138
(801) 524-5030

Mountainous area near Salt Lake City; alpine lakes; streams. Lone Peak Wilderness; High Uintas Primitive Area. Mule deer, elk, moose.

886,374 acres, part in WY. Reservations required for group campsites. Information at ranger stations in Kamas and Salt Lake City, UT, and Evanston and Mountain View, WY. 1,447 campsites, open May/June–Sept./Oct. Food and lodging nearby.

36 Westwater Canyon
Bureau of Land
 Management
P.O. Box M
Sand Flats Rd.
Moab, UT 84532
(801) 259-8193

11 white-water rapids on Colorado River, for experienced boaters only; natural arches; waterfall; historic sites. Varied birdlife includes eagles, Canada geese, ducks, herons.

20 river miles. Apr.–Oct. best time. Entrance fee; permits required; apply 2 months in advance. Information at Westwater Ranger Station, open Apr.-Sept. Primitive camping.

37 Zion N.P.
Springdale, UT
84767
(801) 772-3256

Narrow canyon cut from Navajo sandstone by the Virgin River. Brilliantly colored sandstone and shale formations.

147,035 acres. Spring, fall best times. Entrance fee; permits required for backcountry and for all Virgin River Narrows hikes. Hiking very strenuous. Visitor center: interpretive films, exhibits, programs. Lodge open in summer only; 373 campsites; food services; tram. Food and lodging nearby.

GREEN MOUNTAIN NATIONAL FOREST, VERMONT

Vermont

Cozy villages and friendly ski resorts reflect the human scale of Green Mountain National Forest. The delta wetlands of Missisquoi National Wildlife Refuge afford prime habitat for beavers, muskrats, and waterfowl.

1 **Appalachian N.S.T** *see* Maine

2 **Green Mountain N.F.**
Federal Building
151 West St.
P.O. Box 519
Rutland, VT 05701
(802) 775-2579

New England backcountry of mountains greened by hardwoods. Covered bridges; picturesque valleys; quaint villages. Spectacular fall foliage. 462 miles of trails, including Long Trail and section of Appalachian N.S.T.

295,007 acres. Information at ranger stations in Manchester Center, Middlebury, and Rochester, VT, and Montour Falls, NY. 99 campsites, open May–Sept./Oct./Nov. Food and lodging nearby.

3 **Missisquoi N.W.R.**
R.F.D. 2
Swanton, VT 05488
(802) 868-4781

Unique "bird's-foot" delta ecosystem of extensive wetlands along northeast shore of Lake Champlain; large gatherings of waterfowl, among them goldeneye, mallard, black, ring-necked, and wood ducks; also numerous marsh hawks and colony of great blue herons; summer visitors include rose-breasted grosbeaks and orioles.

5,651 acres. Open dawn to dusk. Late summer–early fall best time. Food and lodging nearby.

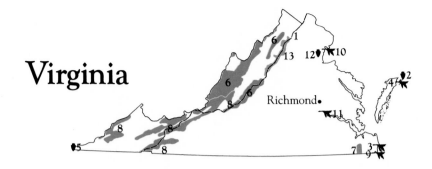

Virginia

Richmond•

The verdant, rolling Blue Ridge Mountains provide the setting for Shenandoah National Park and Virginia's two national forests. From ocean shores roamed by wild Chincoteague ponies to the mysterious Great Dismal Swamp so rich in animal life, the state's five federal refuges differ markedly in environment.

1 **Appalachian N.S.T.**   *see* Maine

2 **Assateague**   *see* Maryland
     Island N.S.

3 **Back Bay N.W.R.**   Dunes, marsh, and timbered upland bounded by the
Bldg. 2, Suite 218   Atlantic Ocean and Back Bay. Wintering snow geese,
Pembroke Office   along with mallards, teal, black ducks, and swans;
     Park   numerous seabirds and shorebirds, including turnstones,
Virginia Beach, VA   sanderlings, and yellowlegs.
23462
(804) 490-0505   4,589 acres. Open dawn to dusk. Fall, winter best times.
Information kiosk. Camping nearby.

4 **Chincoteague**   Beach, marsh, grassland, and pinewoods. Marsh and water
     N.W.R.   birds, shorebirds abundant in summer; otters and sika deer;
Box 62   noted for herd of wild ponies.
Chincoteague, VA
23336   9,460 acres. Open 4 a.m.–10 p.m., Apr.–Oct.; dawn to
(804) 336-6122   dusk, Nov.–Mar. Visitor center at entrance. Food and
lodging nearby.

5 **Cumberland Gap**   *see* Kentucky
     N.H.P.

6 George
  Washington N.F.
210 Federal Bldg.
Harrisonburg, VA
22801
(703) 433-2491

Mountain slopes blanketed with white oak, hickory, and hemlock flanking the broad Shenandoah Valley. Brilliant fall foliage. Fishing streams; waterfalls; wide variety of hiking trails. Civil War sites.

1,054,922 acres, part in WV. Mar.–Nov. best time. Beach use fee. Information at ranger stations in Bridgewater, Buena Vista, Covington, Edinburg, Hot Springs, and Staunton; Massanutten Visitor Center open May–Sept. 807 campsites, many year-round; food services. No drinking water in some areas in winter. Food and lodging nearby.

7 **Great Dismal**
  Swamp N.W.R.
P.O. Box 349
Suffolk, VA 23434
(804) 539-7479

Wooded swamp, habitat of rare plants such as silky camelias and dwarf trilliums; some 200 species of birds, including wood ducks, prothonotary warblers, and pileated woodpeckers; black bears, minks, and bobcats roam here.

102,000 acres, part in NC. Open dawn to dusk. Spring best time. Food and lodging nearby.

8 **Jefferson N.F.**
210 Franklin Rd.
S.W.
Roanoke, VA 24011
(703) 982-6270

Mountains covered with hardwoods interspersed with pine; wild flowers and rhododendrons; outstanding spring, summer, and fall displays. Streams and waterfalls. 300 miles of Appalachian N.S.T.; James River Face Wilderness; Mount Rogers N.R.A.

695,000 acres, part in KY and WV. Information at ranger stations in Blacksburg, Marion, Natural Bridge, New Castle, Wise, and Wytheville. 670 campsites, some open Apr./May–Oct., many year round. No drinking water in White Pine Horse Camp. Food nearby.

9 **Mackay Island**
  N.W.R.

see North Carolina

10 **Mason Neck**
  N.W.R.
14416 Jefferson
  Davis Hwy.
Suite 20A
Woodbridge, VA
22191
(703) 491-6255

Marsh and timberland set aside to protect endangered southern bald eagles; large numbers of pileated woodpeckers in spring; deer and beavers also common.

1,920 acres. Open Apr. 1–Nov. 30, dawn to dusk. Spring, fall best times. Photo blind available by permit. Food and lodging nearby.

11 Presquile N.W.R.
Box 620
Hopewell, VA 23860
(804) 458-7541

Marsh, woods, and farm tracts surrounded by waters of the James River. Sizable flocks of wintering waterfowl, plus spring visitors such as warblers, bluebirds, and vireos; deer also may be sighted.

1,329 acres. Access by refuge-operated ferry; trips must be scheduled 1 week in advance. Open weekdays 7:30 a.m.– 4 p.m. Spring, fall best times. Food and lodging nearby.

12 Prince William Forest Park
P.O. Box 209
Triangle, VA 22172
(703) 221-7181

Former farmland now densely forested with pines and hardwoods. Wildlife includes beavers, raccoons, white-tailed deer. 35 miles of hiking trails; cross-country ski areas.

18,571 acres. Open dawn to dusk. Permits required for backcountry; reservations required for cabins and group camping. Information at park HQ and nature center. Cabins; 191 campsites. Food and lodging nearby.

13 Shenandoah N.P.
Route 4, Box 292
Luray, VA 22835
(703) 999-2243

Abundant wildlife finds refuge in hardwood forests of rolling Blue Ridge Mountains. More than 500 miles of trails, including the Appalachian N.S.T., which parallels the scenic 105-mile Skyline Drive.

194,801 acres. All facilities open in summer, some in spring and fall. Entrance fee; reservations required at Big Meadows, and at Dundo for groups. 2 visitor centers. 2 lodges; 709 campsites; food services. Food and lodging nearby.

SHENANDOAH NATIONAL PARK, VIRGINIA

NORTH CASCADES NATIONAL PARK FROM MOUNT BAKER-SNOQUALMIE NATIONAL FOREST, WASHINGTON

Washington

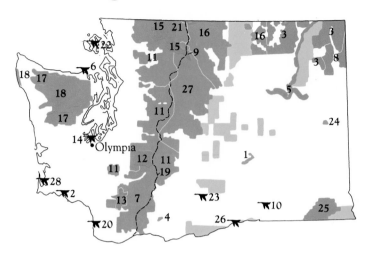

As rain, snow, or glacial ice, water defines and shapes most of the federal lands that embrace nearly one-third of Washington. The nation's greatest single-peak glacial system outside Alaska emanates from majestic Mount Rainier; Olympic and North Cascades National Parks claim dozens of glaciers as well. Snowmelt and abundant rainfall nurture dense forests and luxuriant meadows at lower elevations; large reservoirs account for three national recreation areas. Refuges scattered across the state are noted for varied habitats and diverse wildlife.

1 **Columbia
N.W.R.**
44 S. 8th Ave.
P.O. Drawer F
Othello, WA 99344
(509) 488-2668

Channeled scablands with buttes and mesas, small lakes and streams; managed primarily for wintering waterfowl, mostly mallards, but also other duck species, Canada geese, tundra swans; nesting birds of prey.

22,500 acres. Open daylight hours. Spring, fall best times. Primitive camping. No water available. Food and lodging nearby.

2 **Columbian White-
tailed Deer
N.W.R.**

see Oregon

3 Colville N.F.
U. S. Forest Service
695 S. Main
Colville, WA 99114
(509) 684-3711

Gentle terrain of rolling, timbered mountains, winding, green valleys, and rivers and lakes. Stands of fir, cedar, and spruce. Waterfalls; caves with stalagmites and stalactites. Mushroom gathering and berry picking.

945,052 acres. Reservations required for group camping. Information at ranger stations in Colville, Kettle Falls, Metaline Falls, Newport, and Republic. 346 campsites, open May/June–Sept./Oct. Food and lodging nearby.

4 Conboy Lake N.W.R.
P.O. Box 5
Glenwood, WA 98619
(509) 364-3410

Seasonal lake, forest, and highland meadow below snowcapped Mount Adams. Waterfowl abound in spring; bald eagles common much of the year; coyotes, black-tailed deer, and beavers.

5,500 acres. Open daylight hours. Spring best time. Food and lodging nearby.

5 Coulee Dam N.R.A.
P.O. Box 37
Coulee Dam, WA 99116
(509) 633-1360, x441

Dam impounds waters of the Columbia River in 150-mile-long Franklin D. Roosevelt Lake. Water sports; summer tours of historic Fort Spokane; bird watching.

100,059 acres. May–Oct. best time. Visitor center at Fort Spokane; audiovisual programs, interpretive talks and walks. 328 campsites. Food and lodging nearby.

6 Dungeness N.W.R.
100 Brown Farm Rd.
Olympia, WA 98506
(206) 753-9467

Sandspit with partially wooded upland reaching some 5 miles from Olympic Peninsula into Strait of Juan de Fuca. Superb birding all year, but especially in winter, when visitors include Brandt's cormorants, arctic and red-throated loons, mew gulls, and black turnstones.

572 acres. Walk in only. Open dawn to dusk. Fall, winter best times. Food and lodging nearby.

7 **Gifford Pinchot N.F.**
500 W. 12th St.
Vancouver, WA
98660
(206) 696-7500

Damp, dense conifer forest covering rough terrain that includes Mount St. Helens National Volcanic Monument. Glaciers; streams and lakes; green meadows. Goat Rocks and Mount Adams Wilderness Areas.

1,251,000 acres. Reservations required for group campsites. Information at ranger stations in Amboy, Carson, Packwood, Randle, and Trout Lake. 900 campsites, most open May/June–Sept./Oct. No drinking water in many campgrounds. Food and lodging nearby.

8 **Idaho Panhandle N.F.**

see Idaho

9 **Lake Chelan N.R.A.**
800 State St.
Sedro Woolley, WA
98284
(509) 682-2549

Fjordlike lake in Stehekin Valley, adjacent to North Cascades N.P. Codlike burbot and kokanee salmon in waters 1,400 feet deep. Wildlife also includes deer, mountain goats, bears.

61,890 acres. Access to Stehekin Valley by boat or floatplane; check with HQ for schedule; lower valley accessible early Apr.–mid-Nov. Permits required for backcountry, cross-country, and trail camps; group camping reservations available by mail. Information at ranger stations in Stehekin, Chelan, and Marblemount; interpretive exhibits, guided tours, and programs late June–early Sept. 26 rooms; 50 campsites; food services; tour bus.

10 **McNary N.W.R.**
P.O. Box 239
Umatilla, OR
97882
(503) 922-3232

Open water, wetland, and fields, plus scattered islands in Snake and Columbia Rivers; numerous waterfowl, including migrating ducks and geese in spring and fall; birds of prey such as red-tailed hawks and burrowing owls; coyotes.

3,631 acres. Fall best time. Food and lodging nearby.

11 **Mount Baker-Snoqualmie N.F.**
1022 1st Ave.
Seattle, WA 98104
(206) 442-5400

Thick fir and spruce woods green western slopes of Cascades. Dormant volcanoes; 400 glaciers; alpine lakes; streams and waterfalls; wilderness areas. Heavy rainfall.

2,506,988 acres. Roads impassable in winter. Permits required for Glacier Peak Wilderness; reservations required for group campsites. Information at public service centers in Concrete, Darrington, Enumclaw, Glacier, North Bend, Sedro Woolley, Skykomish, and Verlot. 858 campsites, most open May–Oct. No drinking water in many camping areas. 7 winter sports areas. Food and lodging nearby.

12 **Mount Rainier N.P.**
Tahoma Woods
Star Route
Ashford, WA 98304
(206) 569-2211

Ancient volcano, 14,410 feet high, furrowed by more than 26 glaciers; dense forests; subalpine flowered meadows. Winter sports include snowshoeing. Wildlife watching.

235,404 acres. Nisqually entrance to Paradise open year round; most other park roads closed late Nov.–Apr. Entrance fee; permits required for backcountry use. Longmire Museum; Paradise, Ohanapecosh, and Sunrise visitor centers; illustrated talks, campfire programs. 140 rooms; 596 campsites; food services. Food and lodging nearby.

13 **Mount St. Helens National Volcanic Monument**
Route 1, Box 369
Amboy, WA 98601
(206) 247-5473

Encompasses part of area devastated by the 1980 eruption of Mount St. Helens as well as minimally affected forest areas. Wildlife includes deer and elk. Bird watching.

110,000 acres. June–Oct. best time. Most roads closed by snow in winter. A limited area around volcano is a hazard zone; entry by permit only. Visitor center: daily programs June–Oct. Tour bus. Food and lodging nearby.

14 **Nisqually N.W.R.**
100 Brown Farm Rd.
Olympia, WA 98506
(206) 753-9467

River-delta land fronting Puget Sound attracts migrating shorebirds, seabirds, and waterfowl; western grebes, dunlins, birds of prey, and 19 duck species; bald eagles sometimes sighted.

2,818 acres. Open dawn to dusk. Spring, fall, winter best times. Information kiosk; Twin Barns Education Center for groups by reservation. Photo blind available. Food and lodging nearby.

15 **North Cascades N.P.**
800 State St.
Sedro Woolley, WA 98284
(206) 855-1331

Cascade Range curves northward 700 miles from California to British Columbia. Western slopes moist; eastern, arid. High, jagged peaks; 300 glaciers; waterfalls and lakes.

504,780 acres. Snow prevents access in winter. Permits required for backcountry camping. Information at park offices and ranger stations. Primitive camping.

see California

16 **Okanogan N.F.**
1240 S. 2nd
Okanogan, WA
98840
(509) 422-2704

Isolated, rugged gold rush country. Dense ponderosa pine and Douglas fir forest as well as more open woods. Mountain lakes; alpine meadows; snowcapped peaks; glaciers; Pasayten Wilderness.

1,499,462 acres. July–Oct. best time. Wilderness entry permits required. Information at ranger stations in Okanogan, Tonasket, Twisp, and Winthrop and at Early Winters Information Center. 51 campsites, most open May/June–Sept./Oct. No drinking water in many camping areas. Food and lodging nearby.

17 **Olympic N.F.**
Box 2288
Olympia, WA 98507
(206) 753-9534

Located on Olympic Peninsula and noted for marine climate. Lush rain forests; rugged snowcapped mountains; dense conifer forests; alpine meadows; lakes and streams. Rich vegetation includes mosses, ferns. Roosevelt elk.

649,975 acres. May–Oct. best time. Information at ranger stations in Forks, Hoodsport, Quilcene, Quinault, and Shelton. 379 campsites, most open May–Oct. Food and lodging nearby.

18 **Olympic N.P.**
600 E. Park Ave.
Port Angeles, WA
98362
(206) 452-4501, x230

Snowcapped mountains with 60 active glaciers, rain-forested valleys, and 57 miles of wild and scenic ocean beaches. Wildlife watching, including Roosevelt elk. Wild flowers on Hurricane Ridge in July.

908,720 acres. Very few roads. Permits required for backcountry use; reservations for group camping. Visitor centers in Port Angeles and Hoh Rain Forest; Storm King Visitor Center at Lake Crescent and Kalaloch Visitor Center open only in summer; interpretive and audiovisual programs; winter programs at Hurricane Ridge. Rooms; 1,006 campsites; food services. Food and lodging nearby.

19 **Pacific Crest N.S.T.**   *see* California

20 **Ridgefield N.W.R.**
1309 N.E. 134th St.
Vancouver, WA
98665
(206) 696-7796

Floodplain of Columbia River where large flocks of ducks and geese winter; black-tailed deer roam the refuge, and great blue herons nest close by.

3,100 acres. Open dawn to dusk. Spring, fall, winter best times. Food and lodging nearby.

21 Ross Lake N.R.A.
800 State St.
Sedro Woolley, WA
98284
(206) 873-4500 or
855-1331

Located in the Skagit River Valley, the recreation area divides the north and south units of North Cascades N.P. Named for trapper Alexander Ross, who in 1814 became the first white man to visit this area.

117,574 acres. Permits required for backcountry. Information at ranger stations. 318 campsites; food services. Food and lodging nearby.

22 San Juan Islands N.W.R.
100 Brown Farm Rd.
Olympia, WA 98506
(206) 753-9467

84 rocks, reefs, and small islands in Puget Sound. Birds abound, including tufted puffins, pelagic and Brandt's cormorants, and pigeon guillemots.

Access by ferry or private boat. Only Matia and Turn Islands open to public. Spring, summer best times. Information at Nisqually N.W.R. 24 campsites. Food and lodging nearby.

Snoqualmie N.F.

see **Mount Baker-Snoqualmie N.F.**

23 Toppenish N.W.R.
Route 1, Box 1300
Toppenish, WA
98948
(509) 865-2405

Wetlands, marsh, and fields bordering Toppenish Creek, set aside chiefly as nesting site for waterfowl; quail, pheasants, golden and bald eagles, and coyotes common.

1,764 acres. Open 7:30 a.m.–4 p.m. Spring, fall best times. Food and lodging nearby.

24 Turnbull N.W.R.
Route 3, Box 385
Cheney, WA 99004
(509) 235-4723

Some 100 marshes and lakes interspersed with stands of timber; nesting site for trumpeter swans, Canada geese, 16 duck species; numerous coyotes, white-tailed deer.

15,565 acres. Open dawn to dusk. Spring, summer, fall best times. Photo blind available. Food and lodging nearby.

25 Umatilla N.F.

see Oregon

26 Umatilla N.W.R.

see Oregon

27 Wenatchee N.F.
P.O. Box 811
301 Yakima St.
Wenatchee, WA
98801
(509) 662-4335

Land of jagged peaks; fir and pine stands; canyons; alpine meadows; glacial lakes including 55-mile-long Chelan; semi-arid hills; white-water river. Rare wild flowers. Portions of 3 wilderness areas. Mushroom gathering and berry picking.

1,618,262 acres. Reservations required for American Ridge Ski Bowl camping area. Information at ranger stations in Chelan, Cle Elum, Entiat, Lake Wenatchee, Leavenworth, and Naches. 1,937 campsites, most open May–Oct.; food services. Tour boat on Lake Chelan. 7 winter sports areas. Food and lodging nearby.

28 Willapa N.W.R.
Ilwaco, WA
98624
(206) 484-3482

5 units encompassing Willapa Bay and surrounding sand dunes, marshland, grasslands, and forest. Abundant water birds, black-tailed deer; Roosevelt elk, black bears.

10,000 acres. Open dawn to dusk. Spring, fall, winter best times. Information at Lower Columbia River Refuge Complex, 1309 N.E. 134th St., Vancouver, WA 98665. Camping on Long Island unit; must have own boat. 2 photo blinds available. Food and lodging nearby.

West Virginia

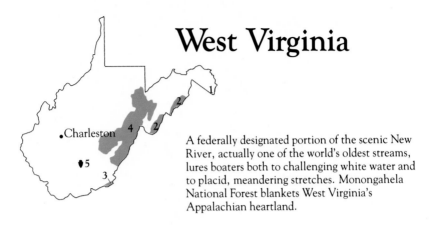

A federally designated portion of the scenic New River, actually one of the world's oldest streams, lures boaters both to challenging white water and to placid, meandering stretches. Monongahela National Forest blankets West Virginia's Appalachian heartland.

1 **Appalachian N.S.T.**   *see* Maine

2 **George Washington N.F.**   *see* Virginia

3 **Jefferson N.F.**   *see* Virginia

4 **Monongahela N.F.**
USDA Building
Sycamore St.
P.O. Box 1548
Elkins, WV 26241
(304) 636-1800

Rich hardwood stands interspersed with conifers. Mountains and high valleys; waterfalls; rock formations; fishing lakes and streams; limestone caves; canyons; white-water river. Includes 4 wilderness areas and Spruce Knob-Seneca Rocks N.R.A.

850,000 acres. Spring, summer, fall best times. Visitor centers at Seneca Rocks and 20 miles east of Richwood; exhibits, interpretive programs. 439 campsites, most open spring to fall, some year round; food services. Food and lodging nearby.

5 **New River Gorge N.R.**
137½ Main St.
P.O. Drawer V
Oak Hill, WV 25901
(304) 465-0508

Flowing north through deep gorges, this 50-mile section of the New River between Hinton and Fayetteville offers opportunities for white-water canoeing and rafting and other water sports.

62,024 acres. Canyon Rim Visitor Center near Fayetteville open year round; Hinton Visitor Center open seasonally. Food and lodging nearby.

Wisconsin

The deeply wooded Apostle Islands, accessible only by boat, welcome solitude-seekers near Lake Superior's southern shore. Noted for fine fishing, lakes and streams by the hundred spangle national forests; a remnant of original prairie grassland survives at Trempealeau National Wildlife Refuge.

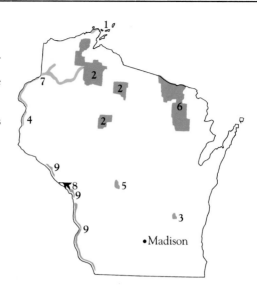

1 **Apostle Islands N.L.**
P.O. Box 729
Bayfield, WI 54814
(715) 779-3397

20 forested islands and an 11-mile coastal strip on the tip of Bayfield Peninsula in Lake Superior. Sandstone cliffs; sandy beaches; high clay banks; historic lighthouses. Excursion boats; chartered fishing trips.

42,009 acres. Access by boat. Permits required for backcountry use; reservations required for group camping. Visitor center; information also at ranger stations. Campsites on islands. Food and lodging nearby.

2 **Chequamegon N.F.**
157 N. 5th Ave.
Park Falls, WI 54552
(715) 762-2461

Gently rolling, forested terrain dotted with more than 400 lakes. Beautiful fall foliage. Good canoeing rivers; Wisconsin Ice Age Trail.

847,000 acres. Mid-Sept.–third week in Oct. for foliage. Reservations required for Sailor Lake group camping area. Information at ranger stations in Glidden, Hayward, Medford, Park Falls, and Washburn. 600 campsites, open May–Sept./Dec.; food services. Food and lodging nearby.

3 **Horicon N.W.R.**
Route 2
Mayville, WI 53050
(414) 387-2658

Marshland noted for huge flocks of ducks and Canada geese in spring and fall; wide variety of birds in spring, summer, and fall includes great egrets, great blue herons, black-crowned night herons, many duck species, pheasants; deer, raccoons, and opossums also thrive.

21,000 acres. Open dawn to dusk. Spring, fall best times. Reservations required for hiking trails in fall. Check with local chambers of commerce about bus and boat tours. Food and lodging nearby.

4 **Lower St. Croix N.S.R.**
P.O. Box 708
St. Croix Falls, WI 54024
(715) 483-3287

27-mile segment of the St. Croix, one of the nation's last unspoiled recreational rivers near a major metropolitan area. Boating, fishing, and camping in a wilderness setting.

8,670 acres, part in MN. May–Sept. best time. Visitor center open in summer. 215 campsites. Food and lodging nearby.

5 **Necedah N.W.R.**
Star Route West
Box 386
Necedah, WI 54646
(608) 565-2551

Mixed habitat of marsh, grass, brush, and forest; noted for flocks of greater sandhill cranes; migrators include geese, ducks, and eagles; wintering site for rough-legged hawks; residents include deer and ruffed grouse. Blueberry picking July 1–Aug. 15.

40,000 acres. Open dawn to dusk; sections closed during hunting and nesting seasons. Spring, summer, fall best times. Information kiosk. Food and lodging nearby.

6 **Nicolet N.F.**
Federal Building
68 S. Stevens
Rhinelander, WI 54501
(715) 362-3415

Working forest providing recreation, watershed, and timber resources. Good fishing streams and lakes. Outstanding scenic drives, especially during fall color displays.

654,000 acres. Information at ranger stations in Eagle River, Florence, Lakewood, and Laona. 624 campsites, most open April/May–Sept./Oct./Dec., a few year round; food services. Food and lodging nearby.

7 **St. Croix N.S.R.**
P.O. Box 708
St. Croix Falls, WI 54024
(715) 483-3287

Some 200 miles of the St. Croix and its tributary, the Namekagon. Rapids provide canoeing adventure. Bird watching.

62,696 acres, part in MN. May–Sept. best time. Visitor centers open in summer. 165 campsites. Launch trips from Taylors Falls daily, June–Oct. Food and lodging nearby.

8 **Trempealeau N.W.R.**
Route 1
Trempealeau, WI
54661
(608) 539-2311

Grassland with lush vegetation. Deer and foxes thrive, along with birds such as woodpeckers, flycatchers, thrushes, and ruffed grouse.

5,617 acres. Open dawn to dusk. Spring, fall best times. Permits required for canoeing in refuge pool. Food and lodging nearby.

9 **Upper Mississippi River National Wildlife and Fish Refuge**

see Minnesota

Wyoming

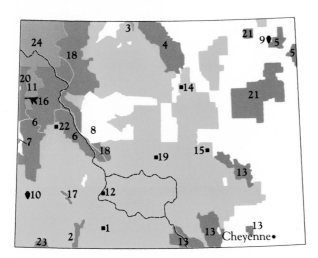

The oldest national park, established in 1872, Yellowstone remains a unifying symbol of natural treasures throughout the United States. Its outstanding geologic features include the world's most extensive system of geysers and other geothermal phenomena; the largest lake in the Rocky Mountains; and a waterfall higher than Niagara's. To the south, Grand Teton National Park enshrines the breathtaking Teton Range—a climber's and skier's paradise overlooking Jackson Hole, famed for its wildlife. National forests, refuges, grasslands, and monuments also contribute superb attractions to the federal domain that comprises nearly half of Wyoming.

| 1 | **Adobe Town** | Isolated area of badlands, sand dunes, and buttes. Wildlife includes pronghorns, mule deer, wild horses and burros, bobcats, coyotes. |

1 Adobe Town
Bureau of Land
  Management
1300 3rd St.
P.O. Box 670
Rawlins, WY 82301
(307) 324-7171

Isolated area of badlands, sand dunes, and buttes. Wildlife includes pronghorns, mule deer, wild horses and burros, bobcats, coyotes.

150,000 acres. July–Sept. best time. 4-wheel-drive vehicle necessary. Primitive camping.

2 Ashley N.F.

see Utah

3 **Bighorn Canyon N.R.A.** — *see* Montana

4 **Bighorn N.F.**
Columbus Bldg.
1969 S. Sheridan Ave.
Sheridan, WY 82801
(307) 672-0751

Mountain country with wide valleys and open alpine meadows; pine and fir stands; glacier; cirques; snowcapped peaks; 300 lakes; canyons; waterfalls; primitive area. Indian medicine wheel and battlefields.

1,107,660 acres. Reservations required for group picnic areas. Information at ranger stations in Buffalo, Greybull, Lovell, Sheridan, and Worland. Lodges; 749 campsites, open June–Sept.; food services. Food and lodging nearby.

5 **Black Hills N.F.** — *see* South Dakota

6 **Bridger-Teton N.F.**
Forest Service Bldg.
340 N. Cache
P.O. Box 1888
Jackson, WY 83001
(307) 733-2752

Forests of pine, spruce, and fir sweep across mountain ranges. Bridger Wilderness: massive outcrops, glaciers, hundreds of lakes and streams. Teton Wilderness: high plateaus, broad valleys, green meadows. Hot springs.

3,400,258 acres. July–Aug. best time. Information at ranger stations in Afton, Big Piney, Jackson, Kemerer, Moran, and Pinedale. 600 campsites, open May/June–Sept./Oct. Food and lodging nearby.

7 **Caribou N.F.** — *see* Idaho

8 **Continental Divide N.S.T.** — *see* Montana

9 **Devils Tower N.M.**
Devils Tower, WY 82714
(307) 467-5370

In 1906 President Theodore Roosevelt named this 865-foot column of hardened magma the first national monument. Tower played important part in Indian folklore.

1,347 acres. Entrance fee. Visitor center open mid-May–Oct. 51 campsites. Food and lodging nearby.

10 **Fossil Butte N.M.**
P.O. Box 527
Kemerer, WY 83101
(307) 877-3450

Rich deposits of freshwater fish fossils, 50 million years old, in what is now a semidesert region.

8,198 acres. Usually closed by snow Nov.–early May. Reservations for accommodations should be made well in advance. Visitor contact station open June–early Sept.; interpretive exhibits. Food and lodging nearby.

11 Grand Teton N.P.
P.O. Drawer 170
Moose, WY 83012
(307) 733-2880

Granite peaks of Teton Range rise precipitously above alpine lakes and the valley of Jackson Hole. Wildlife includes elk, bald eagles, and trumpeter swans. Float trips on Snake River.

310,516 acres. Fall best time. Most facilities closed Oct.–May. Entrance fee; permits required for fishing, climbing, backcountry, boating, and over-snow travel; reservations required for group campsites; registration for off-trail hiking and climbing at Jenny Lake Ranger Station in summer and at park HQ in Moose at other times. Visitor center in Moose; Colter Bay Visitor Center open May–Sept.; exhibits, ranger-led activities. 960 rooms; 929 campsites; food services; tour bus. Food and lodging nearby.

12 Greater Sand Dunes
Bureau of Land Management
P.O. Box 1869
Rock Springs, WY 82901
(307) 382-5350

Soft, windblown sands form one of the largest active dune areas in North America, frequented by elk, mule deer, and pronghorns. Sparse vegetation, mostly sagebrush, grasses.

38,480 acres. June–Sept. best time. Primitive camping.

13 Medicine Bow N.F.
605 Skyline Dr.
Laramie, WY 82070
(307) 745-8971

Mountains, interspersed with broad, open areas, rising out of the high Colorado Plateau. Pine and fir stands; lakes and streams; beaver colonies. Savage Run Wilderness Area.

1,092,000 acres. Information at ranger stations in Douglas, Encampment, Laramie, and Saratoga. 2 lodges; 593 campsites, open May/June–Sept./Oct. Food and lodging nearby.

14 Middle Fork of Powder River
Bureau of Land Management
P.O. Box 670
Buffalo, WY 82834
(307) 684-5586

Middle Fork Canyon southwest of Kaycee. River opens into broad floodplain after cutting through 1,000-foot vertical canyon walls. Wildlife includes elk, bighorn sheep, sage grouse, hawks. Ponderosa pine forest and sagebrush grassland.

48,400 acres. June–Nov. best time. Primitive campsites.

15 **Muddy Mountain**
Bureau of Land Management
951 Rancho Rd.
Casper, WY 82601
(307) 261-5151

Peaks more than 8,000 feet high; gentle slopes covered with aspen, pine, and sagebrush; sparkling streams, home to beavers. Other animals include mule deer, elk, coyotes, golden eagles, hawks.

1,260 acres. Mid–June-Sept. best time. Information at entrance station. 22 campsites. Food and lodging nearby.

16 **National Elk Refuge**
Box C
Jackson, WY 83001
(307) 733-9212

Just northeast of Jackson, refuge provides winter range for about 7,500 elk; other mammals include coyotes, pronghorns, moose, and mule deer; nesting site for trumpeter swans.

24,300 acres. Open dawn to dusk. Winter best time. Sleigh Ride Visitor Center open mid-Dec.–Apr. 1; horse-drawn sleigh tours; exhibits, movies. Food and lodging nearby.

17 **Seedskadee N.W.R.**
P.O. Box 67
Green River, WY 82935
(307) 875-2187

Area along island-dotted Green River and surrounding valley. Sage grouse and birds of prey such as golden eagles and red-tailed and Swainson's hawks.

13,500 acres. Open daylight hours. Late spring, fall best times.

18 **Shoshone N.F.**
W. Yellowstone Hwy.
P.O. Box 2140
Cody, WY 82414
(307) 527-6241

Rugged mountain area blanketed with pine, fir, and aspen. Steep canyons; granite rocks; snowcapped peaks; large glaciers; petrified trees; hundreds of lakes. Grizzly bears. 3 wilderness areas; 2 primitive areas.

2,433,000 acres. High-country areas seldom open before mid-July because of heavy snow. Information at ranger stations in Cody, Dubois, Lander, Meeteetse, and Powell. 374 campsites, open May/June/July–Sept./Oct.; food services. Food and lodging nearby.

19 **Sweetwater Rocks**
Bureau of Land Management
1300 3rd St.
P.O. Box 670
Rawlins, WY 82301
(307) 324-7171

Granite peaks rise 1,200 feet above Sweetwater River; large domes. Sparse vegetation, mostly juniper, Douglas fir, shrubs; mule deer, bighorn sheep.

35,000 acres. Summer best time. Primitive camping. Food and lodging nearby.

20 **Targhee N.F.**

see Idaho

Teton N.F.

see **Bridger-Teton N.F.**

21 **Thunder Basin**
N.G.
809 S. 9th St.
Douglas, WY 82633
(307) 358-4690

High rolling plateaus; upland plains; grasslands with some ponderosa pine. Wildlife includes mountain lions, pronghorns, deer, and golden and bald eagles.

572,319 acres. Sept. best time. No developed campgrounds or recreation areas. To enjoy the area and to avoid trespassing, obtain map from HQ.

22 **Upper Green and**
New Fork Rivers
Bureau of Land
Management
P.O. Box 768
Pinedale, WY 82941
(307) 367-4358

Flowing through scenic lands southeast of Jackson Hole; views of 12,000-foot peaks of Wind River Range; access points. Trout, moose, deer, nesting waterfowl; cottonwoods, willows, pines. Float trips.

100 river miles. Open May–Dec. July–Oct. best time. 4 campsites. Maps necessary to locate access points on public lands and to avoid trespassing on private lands. Food and lodging nearby.

23 **Wasatch N.F.**

see Utah

24 **Yellowstone N.P.**
P.O. Box 168
Yellowstone
National Park,
WY 82190
(307) 344-7381

Our oldest national park, established in 1872, and the largest outside Alaska. More than 300 geysers, including Old Faithful; golden Grand Canyon of the Yellowstone. Wildlife includes black and grizzly bears, moose, bison, more than 225 species of birds.

2,219,823 acres, part in ID and MT. Many roads and all entrances except North closed in winter; access by over-snow vehicle. Entrance fee; permits required for boating and backcountry; reservations for hotels, cabins, lodges, and trailer park. Visitor centers: interpretive and campfire programs. 2,042 rooms; 2,240 campsites; food services; tour bus. Food and lodging nearby.

YELLOWSTONE NATIONAL PARK, WYOMING

GRAND TETON NATIONAL PARK, WYOMING

Index

Acadia N.P. 96
Adobe Town 216
Agassiz N.W.R. 107
Agate Fossil Beds N.M. 125
Alabama 10–11
Alamosa N.W.R. 57
Alaska 12–23
Alaska Maritime N.W.R. 12
Alaska Peninsula N.W.R. 13
Alibates Flint Quarries N.M. 180
Allegheny N.F. 168
Amistad N.R.A. 181
Anahuac N.W.R. 181
Angeles N.F. 38
Angelina N.F. 181
Aniakchak N.M. and Preserve 14
Ankeny N.W.R. 157
Antioch Dunes N.W.R. 39
Apache-Sitgreaves N.F. 25
Apalachicola N.F. 68
Apostle Islands N.L. 213
Appalachian N.S.T. 96
Aransas N.W.R. 181
Arapaho N.F. 57
Arapaho N.W.R. 58
Aravaipa Canyon and Primitive
   Area 25
Arches N.P. 188
Arctic N.W.R. 14
Arizona 24–33
Arkansas 34–37
Arkansas River Canyon 58
Arrowwood N.W.R. 148
Ashley N.F. 188
Assateague Island N.S. 100
Attwater Prairie Chicken N.W.R.
   181
Audubon N.W.R. 148
Aztec Ruins N.M. 137

Back Bay N.W.R. 200
Badlands N.P. 174
Bandelier N.M. 137
Barnegat N.W.R. 135
Baskett Slough N.W.R. 157
Bear Lake N.W.R. 81
Bear River Migratory Bird Refuge
   189
Bear Trap Canyon 117
Beaverhead N.F. 117
Becharof N.W.R. 14
Benton Lake N.W.R. 118
Bering Land Bridge National
   Preserve 14
Bienville N.F. 110
Big Bend N.P. 182
Big Cypress National Preserve 69
Big Lake N.W.R. 34
Big South Fork N.R. and N.R.A.
   177
Big Stone N.W.R. 107
Big Thicket National Preserve 182
Bighorn Canyon N.R.A. 118
Bighorn N.F. 217
Biscayne N.P. 69

Bisti 138
Bitter Lake N.W.R. 138
Bitterroot N.F. 118
Bizz Johnson Trail 39
Blackbeard Island N.W.R. 75
Black Canyon of the Gunnison
   N.M. 58
Black Hills N.F. 174
Black Kettle N.G. 154
Black Ridge Canyons 58
Black Rock Desert 127
Blackwater N.W.R. 100
Block Island N.W.R. 169
Blythe Intaglios 39
Boise N.F. 81
Bombay Hook N.W.R. 67
Bonneville Salt Flats 189
Bosque del Apache N.W.R. 138
Bowdoin N.W.R. 118
Brazoria N.W.R. 182
Breton N.W.R. 94
Bridger-Teton N.F. 217
Brigantine N.W.R. 135
Browns Park N.W.R. 58
Bryce Canyon N.P. 189
Buffalo Gap N.G. 175
Buffalo Lake N.W.R. 182
Buffalo N.R. 34
Burro Creek 26

Cabeza Prieta N.W.R. 26
Cabrillo N.M. 39
Cache N.F. 189
Caddo N.G. 182
Calaveras Big Tree N.F. see
   Stanislaus N.F.
California 38–55
Camas N.W.R. 82
Canaveral N.S. 69
Canyon de Chelly N.M. 26
Canyonlands N.P. 190
Cape Cod N.S. 102
Cape Hatteras N.S. 145
Cape Krusenstern N.M. 14
Cape Lookout N.S. 145
Cape Meares N.W.R. 158
Cape Romain N.W.R. 171
Capitol Reef N.P. 190
Capulin Mountain N.M. 138
Caribou N.F. 82
Carlsbad Caverns N.P. 138
Carlton Pond Waterfowl
   Production Area 97
Carolina Sandhills N.W.R. 171
Carrizozo Malpais 139
Carson N.F. 139
Casa Grande N.M. 26
Catahoula N.W.R. 94
Catoctin Mountain Park 101
Cedar Breaks N.M. 190
Cedar Island N.W.R. 146
Cedar Keys N.W.R. 69
Cedar River N.G. 148
Chaco Culture N.H.P. 139
Challis N.F. 82

Channel Islands N.P. 39
Charles M. Russell N.W.R. 118
Chassahowitzka N.W.R. 69
Chattahoochee N.F. 76
Chattahoochee River N.R.A. 76
Chautauqua N.W.R. 87
Chequamegon N.F. 213
Cherokee N.F. 177
Chesapeake and Ohio Canal
   N.H.P. 101
Chickasaw N.R.A. 154
Chincoteague N.W.R. 200
Chippewa N.F. 107
Chiricahua N.M. 26
Choctaw N.W.R. 10
Chugach N.F. 15
Cibola N.F. 139
Cibola N.W.R. 27
Cimarron N.G. 91
Clear Lake N.W.R. 40
Clearwater N.F. 82
Cleveland N.F. 40
Coconino N.F. 27
Coeur d'Alene N.F. see Idaho
   Panhandle N.F.
Cold Springs N.W.R. 158
Colorado 56–66
Colorado N.M. 59
Columbia N.W.R. 205
Columbian White-tailed Deer
   N.W.R. 158
Colusa N.W.R. 40
Colville N.F. 206
Comanche N.G. 59
Conboy Lake N.W.R. 206
Conecuh N.F. 10
Congaree Swamp N.W.R. 171
Connecticut 66
Continental Divide N.S.T. 119
Coronado N.F. 27
Coulee Dam N.R.A. 206
Crab Orchard N.W.R. 87
Crater Lake N.P. 158
Craters of the Moon N.M. 83
Crescent Lake N.W.R. 125
Croatan N.F. 146
Crooked River N.G. 158
Crosby W.M.D. 150
Cross Creeks N.W.R. 177
Cross Island N.W.R. 97
Cumberland Gap N.H.P. 92
Cumberland Island N.S. 76
Curecanti N.R.A. 59
Curlew N.G. 83
Custer N.F. 119
Cuyahoga Valley N.R.A. 153

Daniel Boone N.F. 93
D'Arbonne N.W.R. 94
Datil Well Campground 140
Davy Crockett N.F. 182
Death Valley N.M. 40
Deer Flat N.W.R. 83
Deerlodge N.F. 119
Delaware 67

Delaware Water Gap N.R.A. 168
Delevan N.W.R. 40
Delta N.F. 110
Delta N.W.R. 95
Denali Highway 15
Denali N.P. and Preserve 15
Des Lacs N.W.R. 150
Deschutes N.F. 159
Deschutes River 159
Desert National Wildlife Range 127
Desolation and Gray Canyons of the Green River 190
DeSoto N.F. 110
DeSoto N.W.R. 90
Devils Lake W.M.D. 150
Devils Postpile N.M. 41
Devils Tower N.M. 217
Diamond Craters Natural Area 159
Dinosaur N.M. 59
District of Columbia 67–68
Dixie N.F. 191
Dominguez-Escalante Ruins 60
Dungeness N.W.R. 206

East Mojave National Scenic Area 41
Eastern Neck N.W.R. 101
Effigy Mounds N.M. 90
Egmont Key N.W.R. 72
El Morro N.M. 140
Eldorado N.F. 41
Erie N.W.R. 169
Eufaula N.W.R. 10
Everglades N.P. 72

Felsenthal N.W.R. 34
Fire Island N.S. 143
Fish Springs N.W.R. 191
Fishlake N.F. 191
Flathead N.F. 119
Flint Hills N.W.R. 91
Florida 68–75
Florissant Fossil Beds N.M. 60
Fort Jefferson N.M. 72
Fort Niobrara N.W.R. 125
Fort Pierre N.G. 175
Fossil Butte N.M. 217
Francis Marion N.F. 172
Franklin Island N.W.R. 97
Fremont N.F. 159

Gallatin N.F. 119
Garnet 122
Gates of the Arctic N.P. and Preserve 15
Gateway N.R.A. 143
George Washington N.F. 201
Georgia 75–78
Gifford Pinchot N.F. 207
Gila Cliff Dwellings N.M. 140
Gila N.F. 140
Glacier Bay N.P. and Preserve 18
Glacier N.P. 122
Glass Butte 159
Glen Canyon N.R.A. 191
Golden Gate N.R.A. 41
Gooding City of Rocks 83
Goshute Canyon Natural

Area 130
Goshute Mountains 130
Grand Canyon N.P. 27
Grand Gulch Primitive Area 194
Grand Mesa-Uncompahgre N.F. 60
Grand River N.G. 175
Grand Teton N.P. 218
Grays Lake N.W.R. 83
Great Dismal Swamp N.W.R. 201
Great Meadows N.W.R. 102
Great Rift 83
Great Sand Dunes N.M. 60
Great Smoky Mountains N.P. 179
Great Swamp N.W.R. 135
Great White Heron N.W.R. 72
Greater Sand Dunes 218
Green Mountain N.F. 199
Greenbelt Park 101
Grimes Point Archaeological Area 130
Guadalupe Mountains N.P. 183
Gulf Islands N.S., Fla. 72
Gulf Islands N.S., Miss. 112
Gunnison N.F. 60

Hagerman N.W.R. 183
Haleakala N.P. 79
Harris Neck N.W.R. 76
Hart Mountain National Antelope Refuge 160
Hatchie N.W.R. 179
Havasu N.W.R. 30
Hawaii 79
Hawaii Volcanoes N.P. 79
Helena N.F. 122
Henry Mountains Buffalo Herd 194
Hiawatha N.F. 104
Hickison Petroglyph Recreation Site 130
Hillside N.W.R. 112
Hobe Sound N.W.R. 73
Holla Bend N.W.R. 34
Holly Springs N.F. 112
Homochitto N.F. 112
Hoosier N.F. 89
Horicon N.W.R. 214
Hot Springs N.P. 35
Hovenweep N.M. 61
Humboldt N.F. 130
Humbug Spires 122
Huron N.F. 104

Idaho 80–86
Idaho Panhandle N.F. 84
Iditarod National Historic Trail 18
Illinois 87–88
Imperial N.W.R. 30
Indiana 89
Indiana Dunes N.L. 89
Innoko N.W.R. 18
Inyo N.F. 42
Iowa 90
Irish Canyon 61
Iroquois N.W.R. 144
Isle Royale N.P. 105
Izembek N.W.R. 18

J. Clark Salyer N.W.R. 150

J. N. "Ding" Darling N.W.R. 73
Jean Lafitte N.H.P. and Preserve 95
Jefferson N.F. 201
Jewel Cave N.M. 175
John Day Fossil Beds N.M. 160
John Day River 160
John Jarvie Historic Site 194
Joshua Tree N.M. 42

Kaibab N.F. 30
Kaniksu N.F. see Idaho Panhandle N.F.
Kansas 91–92
Kanuti N.W.R. 18
Katmai N.P. and Preserve 19
Kenai Fjords N.P. 19
Kenai N.W.R. 19
Kentucky 92–93
Kern N.W.R. 42
Kesterson N.W.R. 42
Key West N.W.R. 73
Kilauea Point Administrative Site 79
King Range National Conservation Area 42
Kings Canyon N.P. 43
Kiowa N.G. 140
Kirwin N.W.R. 91
Kisatchie N.F. 95
Klamath Forest N.W.R. 160
Klamath N.F. 43
Kobuk Valley N.P. 19
Kodiak N.W.R. 19
Kofa N.W.R. 30
Kootenai N.F. 122
Kootenai N.W.R. 84
Koyukuk N.W.R. 20
Kulm W.M.D. 150

Labyrinth Canyon 194
Lacassine N.W.R. 95
Lacreek N.W.R. 175
Laguna Atascosa N.W.R. 183
Lake Alice N.W.R. 150
Lake Andes N.W.R. 176
Lake Chelan N.R.A. 207
Lake Clark N.P. and Preserve 20
Lake Ilo N.W.R. 151
Lake Mead N.R.A. 131
Lake Meredith N.R.A. 183
Lake Woodruff N.W.R. 73
Las Vegas N.W.R. 141
Lassen N.F. 43
Lassen Volcanic N.P. 43
Lava Beds N.M. 46
Lehman Caves N.M. 131
Lewis and Clark N.F. 123
Lewis and Clark N.W.R. 160
Lincoln N.F. 141
Little Bookcliffs Wild Horse Area 61
Little Missouri N.G. 151
Little Sahara Recreation Area 194
Lolo N.F. 123
Long Lake N.W.R. 151
Los Padres N.F. 46
Lostwood N.W.R. 151
Louisiana 94–95
Lower Hatchie N.W.R. 179
Lower Klamath N.W.R. 46

Lower St. Croix N.S.R. 214
Lower Salmon River 84
Lower Suwannee N.W.R. 73
Loxahatchee N.W.R. 73
Lunar Crater Volcanic Field 131
Lyndon B. Johnson N.G. 183

McClellan Creek N.G. 183
McFaddin and Texas Point N.W.R. 186
McKay Creek N.W.R. 160
Mackay Island N.W.R. 146
McNary N.W.R. 207
Madison W.M.D. 176
Maine 96–100
Malheur N.F. 161
Malheur N.W.R. 161
Mammoth Cave N.P. 93
Manistee N.F. 105
Manti-LaSal N.F. 195
Mark Twain N.F. 114
Mark Twain N.W.R. 88
Maryland 100–101
Mason Neck N.W.R. 201
Massachusetts 102–103
Mathews Brake N.W.R. 112
Mattamuskeet N.W.R. 146
Maxwell N.W.R. 141
Medicine Bow N.F. 218
Medicine Lake N.W.R. 123
Mendocino N.F. 46
Merced N.W.R. 46
Merritt Island N.W.R. 74
Mesa Verde N.P. 61
Metcalf N.W.R. 123
Michigan 104–106
Middle Fork of Powder River 218
Mineral Ridge 84
Mingo N.W.R. 114
Minidoka N.W.R. 84
Minnesota 107–109
Minnesota Valley N.W.R. 108
Minnesota Wetlands Complex 108
Missisquoi N.W.R. 199
Mississippi 110–113
Mississippi Sandhill Crane N.W.R. 112
Missouri 114–115
Modoc N.F. 47
Modoc N.W.R. 47
Mono Lake 47
Monomoy N.W.R. 102
Monongahela N.F. 212
Montana 116–124
Monte Vista N.W.R. 61
Montezuma Castle N.M. 30
Montezuma N.W.R. 144
Moosehorn N.W.R. 97
Morgan Brake N.W.R. 113
Morton N.W.R. 144
Mound City Group N.M. 153
Mount Baker-Snoqualmie N.F. 207
Mount Grafton Wilderness Study Area 131
Mount Hood N.F. 161
Mount Rainier N.P. 208
Mount St. Helens National Volcanic Monument 208
Muddy Mountain 219

Muir Woods N.M. 47
Muleshoe N.W.R. 186
Muscatatuck N.W.R. 89

Nantahala N.F. 146
Nantucket N.W.R. 103
National Bison Range 123
National Elk Refuge 219
National Key Deer Refuge 74
Natural Bridges N.M. 195
Navajo N.M. 31
Nebraska 125–126
Nebraska N.F. 126
Necedah N.W.R. 214
Nevada 127–133
New Hampshire 134
New Jersey 135
New Mexico 136–142
New River Gorge N.R. 212
New York 143–144
Nezperce N.F. 85
Nicolet N.F. 214
Ninigret N.W.R. 170
Nisqually N.W.R. 208
Noatak National Preserve 20
North Carolina 145–147
North Cascades N.P. 208
North Dakota 148–152
North Umpqua River 161
Nowitna N.W.R. 20
Noxubee N.W.R. 113

Ocala N.F. 74
Ochoco N.F. 161
Ocmulgee N.M. 76
Oconee N.F. 77
Ogala N.G. 126
Ohio 153
Okanogan N.F. 209
Okefenokee N.W.R. 77
Oklahoma 154–155
Olympic N.F. 209
Olympic N.P. 209
Optima N.W.R. 154
Oregon 156–167
Oregon Caves N.M. 164
Organ Pipe Cactus N.M. 31
Osceola N.F. 74
Ottawa N.F. 105
Ottawa N.W.R. 153
Ouachita N.F. 35
Ouray N.W.R. 195
Owyhee River Canyon 164
Oxbow N.W.R. 103
Oyster Bay N.W.R. 144
Ozark N.F. 35
Ozark N.S.R. 114

Pacific Crest N.S.T. 47
Padre Island N.S. 186
Pahranagat N.W.R. 131
Paiute Primitive Area 31
Panther Swamp N.W.R. 113
Paria Canyon Primitive Area 195
Pariette Wetlands 195
Parker River N.W.R. 103
Pawnee N.G. 64
Payette N.F. 85
Pea Island N.W.R. 147
Pecos N.M. 141

Pee Dee N.W.R. 147
Pelican Island N.W.R. 74
Pennsylvania 168–169
Petit Manan N.W.R. 97
Petrified Forest N.P. 31
Phantom Canyon 64
Phipps-Death Hollow 196
Pictured Rocks N.L. 105
Piedmont N.W.R. 77
Pike N.F. 64
Pilot Peak 132
Pine Forest-Blue Lake 132
Pinnacles N.M. 48
Pipestone N.M. 108
Pisgah N.F. 147
Plumas N.F. 48
Point Reyes N.S. 48
Prescott N.F. 32
Presquile N.W.R. 202
Prime Hook N.W.R. 67
Prince William Forest Park 202
Pungo N.W.R. 147

Quivira N.W.R. 92

Rachel Carson N.W.R. 100
Railroad Grade 196
Railroad Valley W.M.A. 132
Rainbow Bridge N.M. 196
Rainwater Basin W.M.D. 126
Red Rock Canyon Recreation Lands 132
Red Rock Lakes N.W.R. 124
Redwood N.P. 48
Reelfoot N.W.R. 179
Rhode Island 169–170
Rice Lake N.W.R. 108
Ridgefield N.W.R. 209
Rio Grande N.F. 64
Rita Blanca N.G. 186
Rock Creek Park 67
Rocky Mountain N.P. 64
Rogue River 164
Rogue River N.F. 164
Roosevelt N.F. 65
Ross Lake N.R.A. 210
Routt N.F. 65
Ruby Lake N.W.R. 132
Russell Cave N.M. 11

Sabine N.F. 186
Sabine N.W.R. 95
Sachuest Point N.W.R. 170
Sacramento N.W.R. 48
Saguaro N.M. 32
St. Croix N.S.R. 214
St. Francis N.F. 35
St. Joe N.F. see Idaho Panhandle N.F.
St. Marks N.W.R. 74
St. Vincent N.W.R. 75
Salinas N.M. 141
Salinas River W.M.A. 49
Salmon N.F. 85
Salt Meadow N.W.R. 66
Salt Plains N.W.R. 155
Salton Sea N.W.R. 49
Sam Houston N.F. 186
Samuel R. McKelvie N.F. see Nebraska N.F.
San Bernard N.W.R. 187

San Bernardino N.F. 49
San Francisco Bay N.W.R. 49
San Isabel N.F. 65
San Juan Islands N.W.R. 210
San Juan N.F. 65
San Luis N.W.R. 49
San Pablo Bay N.W.R. 52
Sand Lake N.W.R. 176
Santa Ana N.W.R. 187
Santa Fe N.F. 142
Santa Monica Mountains N.R.A. 52
Santee N.W.R. 172
Savannah N.W.R. 77
Sawtooth N.F. and N.R.A. 85
Scotts Bluff N.M. 126
Seedskadee N.W.R. 219
Selawik N.W.R. 20
Seney N.W.R. 106
Sequoia N.F. 52
Sequoia N.P. 52
Sequoyah N.W.R. 155
Shasta-Trinity N.F. 53
Shawnee N.F. 88
Sheldon N.W.R. 133
Shenandoah N.P. 202
Sherburne N.W.R. 108
Sheyenne N.G. 151
Shiawassee N.W.R. 106
Shoshone N.F. 219
Sierra N.F. 53
Silent City of Rocks 86
Siskiyou N.F. 165
Sitgreaves N.F. see Apache-Sitgreaves N.F.
Siuslaw N.F. 165
Six Rivers N.F. 53
Sleeping Bear Dunes N.L. 106
Sleeping Giant/Holter Lake 124
Snake River Birds of Prey Area 86
Snoqualmie N.F. see Mount Baker-Snoqualmie N.F.
Soda Lake 53
South Carolina 171-173
South Dakota 174-176
South Fork of Snake River 86
Square Butte Natural Area 124
Squaw Creek N.W.R. 115
Stanislaus N.F. 54
Steens Mountain Recreation Lands 165
Steese National Conservation Area 21
Stillwater W.M.A. 133
Sullys Hill National Game Preserve 151
Sumter N.F. 172
Sunset Crater N.M. 32
Superior N.F. 109
Sutter N.W.R. 54
Swan Lake N.W.R. 115
Swanquarter N.W.R. 147
Sweetwater Rocks 219

Tahoe N.F. 54
Talladega N.F. 11
Tamarac N.W.R. 109
Target Rock N.W.R. 144
Targhee N.F. 86
Tennessee 177-179

Tennessee N.W.R. 179
Tetlin N.W.R. 21
Teton N.F. see Bridger-Teton N.F.
Tewaukon N.W.R. 152
Texas 180-187
Texas Point N.W.R. see McFaddin and Texas Point N.W.R.
Theodore Roosevelt Memorial Island 68
Theodore Roosevelt N.P. 152
Three Arch Rocks see William L. Finley N.W.R.
Three Rivers Petroglyph Site 142
Thunder Basin N.G. 220
Timpanogos Cave N.M. 196
Tinicum National Environmental Center 169
Tishomingo N.W.R. 155
Togiak N.W.R. 21
Toiyabe N.F. 133
Tombigbee N.F. 113
Tongass N.F. 21
Tonto N.F. 32
Tonto N.M. 33
Toppenish N.W.R. 210
Trempealeau N.W.R. 215
Trinity N.F. see Shasta-Trinity N.F.
Trustom Pond N.W.R. 170
Tule Lake N.W.R. 54
Turnbull N.W.R. 210
Tuskegee N.F. 11
Tuzigoot N.M. 33
Tybee N.W.R. 77

Uinta N.F. 197
Umatilla N.F. 165
Umatilla N.W.R. 165
Umpqua N.F. 166
Uncompahgre N.F. see Grand Mesa-Uncompahgre N.F.
Union Slough N.W.R. 90
Upper Colorado River 66
Upper Green and New Fork Rivers 220
Upper Klamath N.W.R. 166
Upper Mississippi River National Wildlife and Fish Refuge 109
Upper Missouri National Wild and Scenic River 124
Upper Ouachita N.W.R. 95
Upper Souris N.W.R. 152
Utah 188-197
Uwharrie N.F. 147

Valentine N.W.R. 126
Valley City W.M.D. 152
Valley of the Giants Natural Area 166
Vermont 198-199
Virginia 200-203
Voyageurs N.P. 109

Wallowa-Whitman N.F. 166
Walnut Canyon N.M. 33
Wapack N.W.R. 134
Wapanocca N.W.R. 36
Wasatch N.F. 197
Washington 204-211
Washington, D. C. see District of Columbia
Washita N.W.R. 155
Wassaw Island N.W.R. 78
Waubay N.W.R. 176
Wayne N.F. 153
Wenatchee N.F. 211
West Virginia 212
Westwater Canyon 197
Wheeler N.W.R. 11
Whiskeytown-Shasta-Trinity N.R.A. 55
White Mountain N.F. 134
White Mountain N.R.A. 21
White River N.F. 66
White River N.W.R. 36
White Sands N.M. 142
Whitman N.F. see Wallowa-Whitman N.F.
Wichita Mountains N.W.R. 155
Willamette N.F. 167
Willapa N.W.R. 211
William B. Bankhead N.F. 11
William L. Finley N.W.R. 167
Wind Cave N.P. 176
Winema N.F. 167
Wisconsin 213-215
Wolf Island N.W.R. 78
Wrangell-St. Elias N.P. and Preserve 22
Wupatki N.M. 33
Wyoming 216-223

Yaquina Head Natural Area 167
Yazoo N.W.R. 113
Yellowstone N.P. 220
Yosemite N.P. 55
Yukon-Charley Rivers National Preserve 22
Yukon Delta N.W.R. 22
Yukon Flats N.W.R. 22

Zion N.P. 197

Library of Congress CIP Data

Main entry under title:

A Guide to our federal lands.

Includes index.
1. National parks and reserves—United States—Guide-books. 2. United States—Public lands—Guide-books. 3. United States—Description and travel—1981-—Guide-books. I. National Geographic Society (U. S.)
E160.G85 1984   917.3'04927
84-1028

ISBN 0-87044-541-3

A Guide to Our Federal Lands

Published by
The National Geographic
Society

Gilbert M. Grosvenor
President

Melvin M. Payne
Chairman of the Board

Owen R. Anderson
Executive
Vice President

Robert L. Breeden
Vice President,
Publications and
Educational Media

Prepared by
The Special Publications
Division

Donald J. Crump
Editor

Philip B. Silcott
Associate Editor

William L. Allen
William R. Gray
Senior Editors

Staff for this book

Margery G. Dunn
Managing Editor

Penelope Diamanti de Widt
Project Coordinator
and Senior Researcher

John G. Agnone
Picture Editor

Jody Bolt
Art Director

Leslie Allen
William P. Beaman
Barbara Grazzini
Brooke Jennings Kane
Mary R. Lamberton
Louisa V. Magzanian
Writers

Johnna F. Jones
Brooke Jennings Kane
Bonnie S. Lawrence
Researchers

Pamela J. Castaldi
Jennifer Woods
Assistant Designers

Rebecca Bittle Johns
Editorial Assistant

Carol Rocheleau Curtis
Illustrations Assistant

Pamela A. Black
Susan Crosman
Mary Elizabeth Davis
Rosamund Garner
Victoria D. Garrett
Sandra K. Huhn
Artemis S. Lampathakis
Mary Evelyn McKinney
Sheryl A. Prohovich
Kathleen T. Shea
Nancy E. Simson
Linda L. Whittington
Staff Assistants

Map Compilation
and Editing

Timothy J. Carter
Thomas A. Walsh

Map Production

Computer Map Lab,
Cartographic Division

Engraving, Printing,
and Product Manufacture

Robert W. Messer
Manager

George V. White
Production Manager

Gregory Storer
Production Project Manager

Mark R. Dunlevy
David V. Showers
George J. Zeller, Jr.
Assistant Production
Managers

Mary A. Bennett
Production Assistant

Julia F. Warner
Production Staff
Assistant

Composition for A Guide to Our Federal Lands by National Geographic's Photographic Services, Carl
M. Shrader, Director, Lawrence F. Ludwig, Assistant Director. Printed and bound by Holladay-Tyler
Printing Corp., Rockville, Md. Color separations by NEC, Inc., Nashville, Tenn.